EYEWITNESS TRAVEL

TOP 10
GRAN CANARIA

D0229715

LUCY CORNE

DK | Penguin Random House

Top 10 Gran Canaria Highlights

The Top 10 of Everything

CONTENTS

Gran Canaria Area by Area

Streetsmart

Within each Top 10 list in this book, no hierarchy of quality or popularity is implied. All 10 are, in the editor's opinion, of roughly equal merit.

Front cover and spine *Anfi del Mar beach near Arguineguín*
Back cover *Casa de Colón and Catedral de Santa Ana, Las Palmas*
Title page *Village of El Roque, with Roque Bentayga in the background*

The information in this DK Eyewitness Top 10 Travel Guide is checked regularly. Every effort has been made to ensure that this book is as up-to-date as possible at the time of going to press. Some details, however, such as telephone numbers, opening hours, prices, gallery hanging arrangements and travel information, are liable to change. The publishers cannot accept responsibility for any consequences arising from the use of this book, nor for any material on third-party websites, and cannot guarantee that any website address in this book will be a suitable source of travel information. We value the views and suggestions of our readers very highly. Please write to: Publisher, DK Eyewitness Travel Guides, Dorling Kindersley, 80 Strand, London WC2R 0RL, Great Britain, or email travelguides@dk.com

Welcome to
Gran Canaria

Eternal sunshine, beautiful beaches, magnificent mountains, a cosmopolitan capital and a historic heart – Gran Canaria has it all. Whether you're seeking a sub-tropical beach holiday, a city weekend getaway or a world-class hiking destination, with Eyewitness Top 10 Gran Canaria, it's yours to explore.

Gran Canaria is an exciting amalgam of ancient and modern. You'll discover chic cafés in the cobbled streets of **Vegueta**, overlooked by the 15th-century cathedral. You can enjoy creative cuisine in the kitchens of top restaurants, then travel to the whitewashed mountain villages of **Teror** and **Tejeda**, where you'll find menus featuring dishes that have changed little in centuries.

Gran Canaria is a hedonistic hotchpotch of cultures at the crossroads of Europe and the New World. You can walk through the sand dunes of **Maspalomas** at sunrise and imagine you're in the deserts of Africa. Alternatively, listen to Latin music spilling from the bars of **Las Palmas** and wonder if you're in South America, or immerse yourself in one of Europe's liveliest nightspots, in **Playa del Inglés**.

Away from the beaches of its coastline, lies an ancient and mysterious land of sharp-toothed volcanoes, plunging ravines and heart-stirring panoramas. Clouds enshrine **Roque Nublo**, sapphire lakes glisten in the midst of **Tamadaba**'s pine forests, and families still find shelter in the ancient caves of **Barranco de Guayadeque**.

Whether you're coming for a weekend or a week, our Top 10 guide showcases the best of everything Gran Canaria has to offer. There are tips throughout, from seeking out what's free to avoiding the crowds, plus seven easy-to-follow itineraries, designed to tie together a clutch of sights in a short space of time. Add inspiring photography and detailed maps and you've got the essential pocket-sized travel companion. **Enjoy the book, and enjoy Gran Canaria.**

Clockwise from top: **Puerto de Mogán marina; windmill near Mogán; cactuses; Museo Néstor; tiled houses in Puerto de Mogán; Maspalomas sand dunes; Playa Amadores**

Exploring Gran Canaria

Gran Canaria may be small, but there's a lot to take in, and the winding roads of the mountainous interior make for slow progress. These suggested itineraries cover the best of what the island has to offer, and will save you spending precious holiday hours planning routes.

Catedral de Santa Ana is a masterpiece of Canarian architecture.

Two Days in Las Palmas

Day ❶
MORNING

Spend the morning in historic Vegueta, taking in the **Catedral de Santa Ana** (see pp14–15), **Casa de Colón** (see pp12–13), **Museo Canario** (see pp16–17) and the contemporary art gallery **CAAM** (see p76).

AFTERNOON

Head to **Calle Mayor de Triana** (see p77) for shopping. Take a coffee break in **Parque de San Telmo** (see p76). End the day with a cocktail at **La Azotea de Benito** (see p78) and dinner at **Allende Triana** (see p79).

Day ❷
MORNING

Begin in **Parque Doramas**, and then visit the **Museo Néstor** (see p74, closed Mon). Stroll the promenade to Avenida de José Mesa y López for shopping at **El Corte Inglés** (see p77).

AFTERNOON

Dedicate the afternoon to the beautiful sands of **Playa de Las Canteras** (see p73). End the day with tapas and watch the sun set at one of the restaurants behind the beach.

Key

— Two-day itinerary
— Seven-day itinerary

Seven Days in Gran Canaria

Days ❶ and ❷

Follow the two-day Las Palmas itinerary.

Day ❸
MORNING

Start your day in the **Old Quarter of Agüimes** (see p96), and take in the Parroquia de San Sebastián and the **Museo de Historia de Agüimes** (see p44). Spend the rest of the morning in the **Barranco de Guayadeque** (see pp32–3) and lunch in one of the cave restaurants located here.

AFTERNOON

Drive on to pretty **Santa Lucía de Tirajana** (see p103) and have dinner in even prettier **Fataga** (see p100).

Day ❹
MORNING

Drive to **Maspalomas** (see pp20–21) to admire the magnificent sand dunes

The sand dunes at Maspalomas are among Gran Canaria's most unforgettable sights.

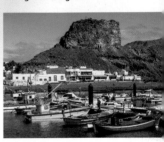

Traditional fishing boats line the harbour at Puerto de las Nieves.

before travelling on to **Puerto de Mogán** *(see pp30–31)*. Enjoy a leisurely lunch by the marina.

AFTERNOON

Take the road inland to Mogán and head to the **Soria reservoir** *(see p57)* before returning to the coast.

Day ❺

MORNING

Make an early start for **Tejeda** *(see pp28–9)*. Explore the town and shop for food before heading to Roque Nublo. Park at Degollada de la Goleta and walk to the site for a picnic.

AFTERNOON

Detour to **Pico de las Nieves** *(see p87)* before ending the day back in **Tejeda**.

Day ❻

MORNING

Book tickets in advance to start your day at the **Cueva Pintada** *(see p81)* in

Gáldar. Afterwards, continue on to **Puerto de las Nieves** *(see pp34–5)* for a seafood lunch.

AFTERNOON

Backtrack to **Agaete** *(see p83)* to take in San Pedro's **Bodega Los Berrazales** *(see p84, closed Sun)* and then sample the local coffee at **Cafeteria Huerto de Las Flores** *(see p85, closed Sat & Sun)*.

Day ❼

MORNING

Beginning in Teror, head straight to the **Basílica de Nuestra Señora del Pino** *(see pp26–7)*, and then drive on to **Arucas** *(see pp82–3)*. Photograph the church, tour the rum factory and enjoy lunch at **Casa Brito** *(see p85, closed Sun D, Mon & Tue)*.

AFTERNOON

Spend a couple of hours in the **Jardín Botánico Viera y Clavijo** *(see pp18–19)* and end with a breathtaking drive to **Caldera de Bandama** *(see p95)*.

Top 10 Gran Canaria Highlights

Colourful boats in the marina at Puerto de Mogán

🔟 Gran Canaria Highlights

Gran Canaria has often been described as "a continent in miniature", and with good reason. Within just 1,500 sq km (580 sq miles) you can travel from the rugged northern coast through verdant laurel forests and extinct volcanoes to the central peaks, before you descend again through ancient pine woodlands and reach glorious golden beaches in the south.

1 Casa de Colón

Trace Columbus's journeys in this museum set in the 15th-century governor's house where the explorer is said to have stayed en route to the New World *(see pp12–13)*.

2 Catedral de Santa Ana

Las Palmas's cathedral has been an emblem of the city since the Spanish Conquest. Its construction over 400 years explains the range of styles that make it one of the island's most important artistic monuments *(see pp14–15)*.

3 Museo Canario

Since they died out soon after the Spanish Conquest, little is known about how the Guanches (early Canarios) lived. Gain insight at the Museo Canario *(see pp16–17)*.

4 Jardín Botánico Viera y Clavijo

Spain's largest botanical garden is a mix of endemic and tropical plants. Giant lizards bask in the sun, while songbirds chirrup in the laurel and pine plantations *(see pp18–19)*.

5 Maspalomas

With its golden dunes, this is both a tourist resort and an area of stunning natural beauty, visited by holidaymakers and migrating birds alike *(see pp20–21)*.

Puerto
las Nie
🔟
Ag

El Risco
GC-200
Parque Natu
de Tama

Puerto de
la Aldea
GC-210
San Nicolás
de Tolentino
El Carri

Parque
del N

Tásarte

Veneguera
GC-200
Moga

8 Puerto
de Mogán

Puerto Rico
GC-S
El

Teror ⑥

Set in an area of outstanding natural beauty, this quiet, architecturally exquisite Canarian town has deep historical roots *(see pp24–5)*.

⑦ Tejeda

Drama and beauty combine forces in this picturesque village, where pavement cafés spill onto cobbled streets above the ravine *(see pp28–9)*.

Puerto de ⑧ Mogán

Sunshine and glorious sunsets are the trademark of this, the island's prettiest resort. Straddling canals, it's known as Little Venice *(see pp30–31)*.

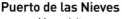

0 kilometres 8

0 miles 8

⑨ Barranco de Guayadeque

Guanche cave homes and modern troglodyte abodes line the sides of this stunning ravine *(see pp32–3)*.

Puerto de las Nieves ⑩

Many visitors pass through en route to Tenerife, but this pretty fishing village is a destination in its own right. Watch the boats, enjoy a seafood lunch, and unwind *(see pp34–5)*.

TOP 10 ⭐ Casa de Colón, Las Palmas

One of the capital's most delightful buildings is a wonderful museum where the main focus is the discovery of America. In the 15th century, the governor's home stood on this site, though the building has changed considerably since then. While not certain, it's very likely that this is where Christopher Columbus stayed in 1492 before he set off in search of a shortcut to India and unwittingly stumbled across America instead.

1 Historical Las Palmas

Children love the interactive model of late-17th-century Las Palmas **(right)**. There are also models of the Castillo de la Luz and Rejón's settlement of 1478.

2 Pre-Columbian Art

The crypt contains some remarkable reproductions of Mexican and Ecuadorian pottery from 500 BC to the 10th century. Most are idols, while others are decorative pieces.

3 Reproduction of La Niña

Be transported back to the 15th century in this replica of *La Niña*, said to have been Columbus's favourite ship. Of special note is the voyager's cabin, complete with a painting and crucifix from the original vessel.

4 Façade

If you view the museum from the cobbled streets around it, you can spot details of Las Palmas's earliest architecture – parts of the façade date from the 1500s. However, the current building **(below)** bears little resemblance to the original structure.

5 Canarian Emigration

Once the transatlantic route was established, Canarians started emigrating in their hundreds. Paintings and information panels tell the story of the exodus and of the trades that thrived then failed.

6 The Discovery

You can trace the four journeys Columbus made across the Atlantic on maps of his version of the world. A reproduction of his diary lies open at the page detailing his first stop in the Canary Islands, when he came ashore at Las Palmas and La Gomera before crossing the ocean.

7 Early Navigation

See absorbing old maps, atlases and a rare 16th-century bronze astrolabe **(left)**. Trace the changing perceptions of the world from Ptolemy's sophisticated 2nd-century map through to increasingly accurate efforts in the 1500s.

LOVE ON THE HIGH SEAS?

Some historians suggest that there was more on Columbus's mind than favourable winds when he chose to pass through the Canaries. The decision to stop at La Gomera, rather than the larger Tenerife, to stock up on supplies, fuelled suspicion that he was visiting his lover Beatriz de Bobadilla, a member of the Spanish court.

8 Historic Paintings

A whistle-stop tour through 500 years of art starts with early religious paintings **(below)**. Make sure you visit the room dedicated to Canarian artists, with colourful 20th-century landscapes and a painting by local artist Néstor de la Torre.

Museum Floorplan

Key to Floorplan
- 1st floor
- Ground floor
- Basement

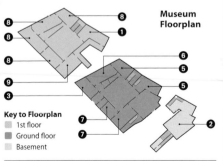

9 Model and Maps of the Island

Plan your stay using a 3D model showing ravines, craters and mountains – an up-to-date view of the island's topography.

10 Ceilings and Courtyards

The reproduction Mudéjar ceilings are very impressive. Upstairs is the only original section that is ornately carved.

NEED TO KNOW

MAP M5 ■ C/Colón 1 ■ 928 31 23 73 ■ www.casadecolon.com

Open 10am–6pm Mon–Sat, 10am–3pm Sun. Adm: €4.00

Guided tours are available on request.

■ Restaurante Marsala on C/Mendizábal is a popular upmarket spot for lunch.

■ Don't forget to visit the Ermita de San Antonio Abad, 50 m (164 ft) from the museum. Columbus is said to have prayed here before his journey across the Atlantic.

TOP 10 ⭐ Catedral de Santa Ana, Las Palmas

Dominating the Vegueta skyline, the cathedral's twin bell towers are the most recognizable landmark of Las Palmas. Construction started just 14 years after the Spanish conquered Gran Canaria, but additions continued to be made late into the 19th century. The result is a microcosm of Canarian architecture: Gothic, Neo-Classical, Renaissance and local styles are all represented. Though this massive edifice differs wildly from the original, remnants of the 15th-century structure are still visible.

1 Chapels
You can see the preserved body of Bishop Buenaventura Codina in the Capilla de los Dolores. Of the other ten chapels, the Capilla de San Fernando, with the cathedral's only Baroque altarpiece, stands out.

2 Ceiling
Admire the intricate Gothic ceiling **(above)**. High above the altar are wooden statues of the apostles.

3 Patio de los Naranjos
Entered via the Puerta del Aire, this leafy 17th-century courtyard joins the cathedral to the Museum of Sacred Art. Built in a typical Canarian manner, it is overlooked by wooden balconies.

4 Façade
Aping the original Gothic design, the impressive Neo-Classical façade **(right)** was added in the 19th century. From inside you can clearly see the join between the two.

5 Tombs
The grand tomb of local politician Fernando de León y Castillo, in the Capilla de Santa Teresa, was built by Miguel de la Torre in 1928. Historian and naturalist José de Viera y Clavijo, one-time archdeacon of Fuerteventura, has a more modest tomb in the Capilla de San José.

6 Square and Statues
Guarding the cathedral and the square in which it stands are eight statues depicting the dogs **(below)** that supposedly gave the Canary Islands their name. Among the other grand buildings that line the large plaza are the episcopal palace and the old town hall.

7 Museo Diocesano de Arte Sacro
Adjoining the cathedral is the Museum of Sacred Art, a collection of religious art that includes sculptures, paintings and woodcarvings dating back to the 16th century. Presiding over the Chaplain's Room is an important Luján Pérez crucifix, which leaves the confines of the cathedral once a year to appear in the city's Easter procession.

8 Viewing Terrace

Jump into the lift that whizzes you up to the cathedral's bell tower to enjoy fine views over the old town, commercial district and port **(above)**. A lively commentary gives a brief history of Las Palmas.

JOSÉ LUJÁN PÉREZ

Born in Santa María de Guía, Luján Pérez (1756–1815) was Gran Canaria's most prolific and respected religious sculptor. Venerated for his ability to create perfectly proportioned figures, he favoured sculptures of Christ or the Virgin Mary. Admire his intricate Baroque carvings in churches across the island, though his finest works are to be seen in its leading places of worship, the cathedral and the Basílica de Nuestra Señora del Pino in Teror (see pp24–5).

NEED TO KNOW

MAP M5 ■ C/Obispo Codina 13 ■ 928 31 49 89

Museo Diocesano de Arte Sacro: C/Espíritu Santo 20. 10am–4:30pm Mon–Sat. Adm: €3.00

■ Find cafés and bars on nearby C/Pelota.

■ Entrance to the cathedral is via the Museo Diocesano de Arte Sacro on Calle Espíritu Santo. Mass is said two times daily Mon–Fri at 8:30am and 9:30am, once on Sat at 7pm and four times on Sun at 10am, noon, 1pm and 7pm.

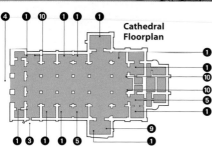

Cathedral Floorplan

9 Sculptures

The cathedral's most significant sculpture is a Luján Pérez masterpiece, *Nuestra Señora de los Dolores* ("Our Lady of Sorrows"), housed in the chapel of the same name. It accompanies a statue of Christ in the annual Easter parade.

10 Paintings

Baroque paintings by Canarian maestro Juan de Miranda flank the altar. Juan de Roelas's canvas in the Capilla de Santa Catalina is typical of 17th-century Sevillian art.

TOP10 ⭐ Museo Canario, Las Palmas

Early Canarian history is a mysterious and fascinating subject that is given in-depth coverage in this excellent museum. The collection presents the most respected theories concerning the origins and practices of the Guanches, allowing you to reach your own conclusions. While most of the objects were unearthed on Gran Canaria, there is also a lot of detailed information on the primitive cultures of the other islands.

1 Pintaderas
The purpose of these small ceramic stamps still isn't known. Guanches used them either to mark patterns on their skin or to personalize grain stores. Pick your favourite and then head to the shop for a replica necklace.

2 Funeral Rites and Medicine
With mummification just for the higher classes, the Guanches also built stone tombs and wooden coffins. Ghoulish skulls illustrate trepanation, a medical procedure in which cranial holes were drilled to ease pain.

3 Skulls and Bones
Hundreds of smiling skulls, possibly of Cro-Magnon man, adorn the walls in this eerie yet intriguing room (above).

4 Housing
The Spaniards were intrigued to find primitive peoples living in caves and stone houses alongside more advanced communities. Fascinating photos and models (below) illustrate both types of dwelling.

5 Aboriginal Ceramics
This island-by-island showcase of aboriginal ceramics also includes the primitive tools used to create them.

⑥ Mummies

Some theories link the Guanches to the Egyptians, owing to their similar methods of mummification **(above)**. Archeologists continue to find artifacts across the islands, but the tombs were raided long ago, and their contents sold to the museum.

Key to Floorplan
- First floor
- Ground floor

⑩ Magic and Religion

Chroniclers of the Conquest wrote that the Guanches worshipped a single god, but the survival of numerous idols suggests that this was not the case. Most deities found on the island take the female form; the largest, the Tara Idol, is now a symbol of pride for Canary Islanders.

⑦ Reproduction of the Cueva Pintada

The original site is in Gáldar, but you can also see some Guanche art at the museum. The geometric patterns in black, white and red represent the finest examples of cave art to be seen on the islands. The museum's version is an almost perfect replica of the original.

⑧ Agriculture and Farming

The basic tools on display demonstrate the tough life of the pastoral Guanches, who survived on limited resources.

⑨ Traditional Pottery

The tradition of crafting pottery without using a wheel has persisted on Gran Canaria. See some examples here **(right)**.

NEED TO KNOW

MAP L5 ■ C/Dr Verneau 2
■ 928 33 68 00 ■ www.elmuseocanario.com

Open 10am–8pm Mon–Fri, 10am–2pm Sat, Sun

Adm: €4.00; concessions €2.40; children under 12 free

■ The museum shop is located on the right-hand side, just before you enter the museum. It sells handicrafts, books and a selection of souvenirs.

■ For those who want to delve deeper into Canarian history, the museum has a superlative library, which holds almost every book published in or about the Canary Islands, as well as a huge archive of Canarian newspapers.

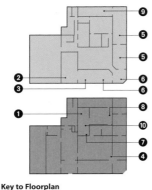

TOP 10 ⭐ Jardín Botánico Viera y Clavijo

Nestled in the Guiniguada ravine, Spain's largest botanical garden is in Tafira Alta, 7 km (4 miles) from Las Palmas. Its steep paths are cloaked in Macronesian flora, both endemic and imported. Showcasing all the flora of the Canary Islands over the six decades of the garden's existence, it is one of Gran Canaria's most prized attractions. Although pretty in any season, the best time to visit is in January or February, after the winter rains have worked their magic.

El Alpendre ①
Built in traditional Canarian style, this stone farm shed **(right)** pre-dates the surrounding gardens. Restored in 1989, it holds a thresher, silo, plough and other agricultural articles.

② **Cactuses and Succulents**
The lowest part of the garden is home to an impressive array of cactuses **(below)**, of both native and imported species. There are around 2,000 varieties of succulent plant on display in this section, almost a third of the world's known species.

Map of Jardín Botánico Viera y Clavijo

③ **Waterlilies**
The official meeting point, the waterlily pond of the pretty Plaza de los Nenúfares is also the site of permanent and temporary exhibitions on different aspects of the garden.

④ **Fountain of the Wise**
This basalt monument pays tribute to important local botanists. A panel lists plant species beside the discoverers who named them.

⑤ **Pine Wood**
If you don't manage to visit a Canarian pine forest, at least breathe in the scent of pine trees here. In spring, look out for the blossoms of the Canary gum.

7 Islands Garden

Get an overview of the plant life of all seven islands, including some rare species. The plants are grouped by island of origin **(left)**.

8 Laurel Forest

Until the last ice age, much of Europe was covered in laurel forest *(laurisilva)*; the only surviving examples are in the Canary Islands and Madeira. An area of the garden was planted with *laurisilva* in 1964. Within it are some rare species, including the Garoé tree, sacred to the original inhabitants of El Hierro.

9 Plaza de Viera y Clavijo

The first port of call for visitors using the upper entrance is this small square, overlooked by a bust of 18th-century historian and naturalist José de Viera y Clavijo. The view of the gardens from here gives you a sneak preview of what's in store.

10 Exhibition Centre

If you want to know more about Canarian flora, the small exhibition centre has information on the many habitats found on the Canary Islands. Audiovisual and interactive exhibits add to the information provided in the wall displays.

6 Lost Dragons

A subspecies of the legendary *Draecaena draco* (or dragon tree), the *Draecaena tamaranae* **(below)** was discovered on Gran Canaria in 1972. One of the rarest trees in the world, its sap runs red and is known as dragon's blood.

ROOTS AND BRANCHES

Swedish botanist Eric Sventenius set up the garden in 1952, aiming to create a space where people could enjoy plants from across the islands without needing to get on a boat. The garden opened to the public in 1959. After the death of Sventenius in 1972, British naturalist David Bramwell took over the reins, and began to develop the garden as an investigative centre, as well as a public park. Today, it has an international reputation as a conservation and research centre, conducting important studies into the unique flora of the Canaries.

NEED TO KNOW

MAP E2 ■ GC-310 & GC-110 ■ 928 21 95 80 ■ www.jardincanario.org

Open Apr–Sep: 9am–7:30pm daily; Oct–Mar: 9am–6pm daily

Exhibition Centre: 9am–2:30pm Mon–Fri

■ The gardens are a popular venue for wedding photos, so you may spot a bride and groom posing in among the plants and flowers.

■ The gardens have two entrances. The first is on the GC-310 (lower entrance), while the second is on the GC-110 (upper entrance).

■ Disabled visitors can enter by the lower gate on the GC-310. Much of the garden isn't accessible, but the lower section is step-free.

🔟⭐ Maspalomas

Maspalomas is best known for its magnificent sand dunes, protected as a nature reserve. Part of the original expanse was destroyed in a flurry of construction in the 1960s and 1970s; many plant and animal species were lost at that time, but the authorities are working to reintroduce them. Today Maspalomas is one of the Canary Islands' largest resorts, but it's still easy to find a peaceful spot in which to enjoy the sun away from the tourist crowds.

Sand Dunes
Contrary to popular belief, these 400 ha (988 acres) of golden sand **(right)** didn't blow across from the Sahara Desert; they washed up from the ocean. While a large part is constantly on the move, there is a stable section, home to a variety of flora and bird life. Stick to the signed routes to protect the wildlife.

② The Resort
The area is still best known as a major tourist resort favoured by northern Europeans. Maspalomas was a victim of the construction boom, but it is a far more exclusive resort than its raucous neighbour Playa del Inglés.

③ Maspalomas Beach
This is the island's supreme beach **(below)**. Families favour the calm seas by the lighthouse. The section by Playa del Inglés is nudist.

④ Mirador
You'll get some very fine views from the *mirador* (viewing point) on the main road to neighbouring Playa del Inglés. It is very popular among tourists.

⑤ Golf Course
Unrivalled weather and vistas of the dunes and ocean beyond make Maspalomas' golf course special. Non-members are welcome.

NEED TO KNOW

MAP D6

Parque Botánico de Maspalomas: 10am–6pm daily

Golf greens: Adm: €64.00 (summer), €109.00 (winter)

Camel rides: Camello Safari Dunas. 928 76 07 81. 9am–4pm daily. Adm: adults €12.00; children €8.00

■ *Chiringuitos* (kiosks selling snacks and drinks) are dotted around the beach. You can also take a picnic and lunch on a bench next to the lagoon.

■ Visit the dunes in the early morning or late evening to avoid burning your feet.

7 Camel Rides

Pretend you really are in the desert as you ride through the dunes on the back of a dromedary **(left)**. Trips leave from the east side of the ravine, north of the lagoon. A half-hour ride takes you through areas thick with daisies and tamarisk.

CONSERVATION, NOT CONSTRUCTION

Today, local government is attempting to repair the havoc wreaked by mass construction, with schemes to reintroduce bird and plant species once common in the area. Not so long ago, the priority was to profit from the dunes at all costs, even if it meant approving projects that would inevitably damage the fragile ecosystem. The demolition of a half-built hotel in the dunes in 1989 was a turning point in saving Gran Canaria's most notable landscape from total destruction.

9 Lighthouse

Standing in a square is one of the island's most striking landmarks: a 55-m (180-ft) lighthouse **(right)**. It was built in the 19th century.

6 Bird-Watching

As well as local species, many migrating birds use the site as a pit stop. In spring and autumn look out for kingfisher, heron, curlew and egret, along with the usual nesting birds – kestrel, plover and moorhen. Less common species include osprey, courser and grey duck.

8 Parque Botánico de Maspalomas

Open daily and free to enter, Maspalomas' vast botanical garden spreads across 12,000 sq m (129,000 sq ft). It is home to more than 500 species of flora. The park also operates tours for nature enthusiasts and visitors.

10 Lagoon and Palm Grove

Palm trees from this ancient grove were sent to California in the 18th century. Look out for mullet, guppies and bream in the murky waters of the small lagoon nearby.

Map of Maspalomas

GC-1
SAN FERNANDO
GC-500
GC-1
2
8
5
PLAYA DEL INGLÉS
Playa del Inglés
MASPALOMAS
7
4
MELONERAS
Dunas de Maspalomas
6
10
Playa de el Faro
Playa de Maspalomas
9
3
1

🔟⭐ Teror

A visit to Teror is a must, not only for its exquisite Canarian architecture, but also because of its historic and religious importance. An independent parish since 1514, Teror is one of the oldest urban centres on the island. Its religious connections date back to the time when the Virgin Mary was sighted under a pine tree in a nearby forest. The Madonna of the Pine later became the island's patron saint, and pilgrims travel from near and far to pay homage. The town centre was declared a heritage sight in 1979.

Calle Real de la Plaza ①

If you appreciate Canarian architecture, you'll love this peaceful street **(right)**, with its traditional balconies and red-tiled roofs.

② Market

Gran Canaria's oldest market offers a curious blend of traditional foodstuffs, bric-a-brac and religious memorabilia. The stall-holders set up behind the church on Sundays, livening up the otherwise eerily quiet town.

③ Plaza Teresa de Bolívar

Built in 1953 as an overspill for the Fiesta del Pino, this square **(below)** was dedicated to Teresa de Bolívar, wife of the South American revolutionary Simón Bolívar. Her family come from Teror, and the family crest adorns the square.

④ Cistercian Convent

The nuns at this convent sell home-made cakes. Ring the bell, and a turn-table will rotate, showing what's on offer. Place your money on the turntable and voice your preference. An unseen nun will pass your cakes over.

⑤ Chorizo de Teror

Garlic lovers will adore the tasty local sandwich-filler. This flavoursome, spreadable sausage is available at every bar and restaurant, and also at the Sunday market.

⑥ Finca de Osorio

Set in the lush Parque Rural de Doramas, this farm boasts some unique flora, such as the pretty Canarian bellflower. Visitors can look out for shrews and owls, and take in fine views from the top of Pico de Osorio, the Finca's famous peak.

Previous pages The palm-lined beach at Amadores

8 Casa de los Patronos de la Virgen

Teror's main museum **(left)** offers a glimpse into how the Canarian gentry lived in years gone by. Delightfully furnished rooms and a small chapel encircle the patio, which has an Italian fountain as its centrepiece. The place is wonderfully authentic, right down to the musty smell that still lingers.

9 Casa de la Cultura (Episcopal Palace)

Part of this magnificent building is still home to the bishop, but a large section is used for temporary exhibitions by local artists. This is fitting, as it was the townsfolk who presented the house to the Canarian bishops in the 18th century, in gratitude for their support in building the basilica.

Fiesta del Pino 7

On 8 September each year, Teror becomes a hive of activity. Pilgrims walk from all over the island to join in the festivities in honour of their patron saint **(right)**.

THE GREEN HEART OF GRAN CANARIA

Teror boasts areas of natural beauty, which have earned it the title *el corazón verde de Gran Canaria* ("the green heart of Gran Canaria"). Thanks to considerable winter rainfall, the region has lush ravines, palm groves and an area of rare laurel forest. Above the town, the Caldera de Pino Santo (Holy Pine Crater) and its environs have been declared a protected landscape in recognition of their natural beauty.

Map of Teror

10 Basílica de Nuestra Señora del Pino

Home to the Madonna of the Pine, this church *(see p26–7)* is a significant island highlight.

Basílica de Nuestra Señora del Pino

The basilica's ornate altarpiece, seen from the nave

1 Main Altarpiece

Ornately carved from dark wood, the main altarpiece is the work of Nicolás Jacinto, and is considered the finest example of Rococo art on the island. Crowned with the Virgin's ornate silver throne, and with a glorious silver frontispiece decorating its lower section, it outshines all its competitors.

Floorplan of Basílica de Nuestra Señora del Pino

2 Nuestra Señora del Pino

For hundreds of years, the faithful have embroidered the flamboyant cloaks that adorn the Virgin. Beneath the gowns stands a wooden Gothic sculpture from the late 1500s or early 1600s. The theft in 1975 of a selection of precious stones from her crown is still a sore point among locals. For a close look at this statue, enter through the basilica's *camarín* (shrine).

3 Treasure Room

This is where you can really get to grips with the importance the Madonna has for the people of the island. The room contains a bizarre selection of gifts from the faithful. An adjoining room shows the Virgin's many outfits, some of which date back to the 18th century. She dons a different dress each year during the Fiestas del Pino *(see p25).*

Pope Pius XII stained glass

4 The Crucified

This eerily lit image of Christ on the cross is another Luján Pérez piece, dating back to 1790. It is one of his best works.

5 Other Statues

Noteworthy sculptures in the basilica also include a marvellous image of St Matthew clutching a crucifix, and a gold-plated image of St Ramón Nonato. The most recent statue is *The Sacred Heart of Jesus,* which dates from the early years of the 20th century.

6 Stained-Glass Windows

Amongst the finest examples is an image of Pope Pius X from 1914, when the Virgin of the Pine was named Gran Canaria's patron saint. The window is on the main façade, along with an impressive image of Pope Pius XII.

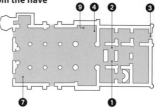

THE HOLIEST STATUE

On 8 September 1481, the Virgin Mary appeared to Juan Frías, bishop of Gran Canaria, in the branches of a pine tree. He could never have guessed how venerated that image of her would become. A statue of the Madonna was enshrined in a small church in the centre of Teror. Since then, the devoted have revered Nuestra Señora del Pino (Our Lady of the Pine). The original church has been replaced twice, and has gradually grown into the huge edifice we see today. It has become an important pilgrimage site, and there is an annual two-day festival, which culminates in an evening procession on 8 September.

TOP 10
BIZARRE GIFTS TO THE MADONNA

1 Football signed by the Las Palmas team

2 Broken watch

3 British pound note with message asking for help

4 Toy car

5 Sports trophies

6 Academic certificates

7 Well-loved teddy

8 Garish souvenir-style statuettes

9 Specially composed poems to her

10 Military medals

Nuestra Señora del Pino is the patron saint of Gran Canaria; her statue is paraded through the streets of Teror on 8 September.

7 Altar of Souls

The least flamboyant of the church's altars is perhaps also its most striking, with its weathered painting of souls anguishing in purgatory.

8 Rescued Relics

Two relics remain from previous incarnations of the church: a large stone font from the first, 16th-century chapel, now in the *camarín*; and, in the treasure room, a cross fashioned from the pine tree where the vision of the Virgin was first seen.

9 Christ Tied to a Column

The main focus of Teror's Easter parades is an anguished statue carved by Luján Pérez in 1793. Considered one of his finest works, the image is flanked by statues of St Michael and the Resurrection, also from the late 18th century.

10 The Building

Little remains of the previous churches erected on this site. The octagonal tower was a feature of the 17th-century building; the present (1767) tower is a replica.

The basilica's imposing façade

TOP 10 ⭐ Tejeda

Nestling in the folds of a magnificent Caldera, Tejeda is one of Gran Canaria's prettiest mountain villages. The island's earliest inhabitants occupied this area from the 3rd century, and this was their last stronghold against the Spanish invaders in 1483. Within striking distance of so many important ancient sites, this is a great base for exploring. Tejeda is famous for its almond trees, and specializes in almond products such as *bienmesabe* (a sweet, sponge-based dessert) and *mazapanes* (marzipan cakes).

1 Roque Nublo
The Canaries' most famous rock **(below)** is part of a volcanic chimney. Follow the path from the road to the "Cloud Rock", or snap it from anywhere in the interior.

2 Cuevas del Rey
No one knows if the man-made "Caves of the King", which were carved out of the west face of Roque Bentayga, were used by monarchs. The largest is called Cueva del Guayre.

5 Almond Blossom
In February the Tejeda valley is awash with almond blossom, heralding spring and the Fiesta del Almendro en Flor, one of the island's prettiest fiestas.

3 Pico de las Nieves
The view from this peak **(left)** of 1,949 m (6,394 ft) is marred by the presence of a military radio station, but on a clear day you'll still enjoy fine panoramas down to the coast.

4 Roque Bentayga
Transport yourself to the Stone Age by exploring this pre-Hispanic site. Offerings and sacrifices were probably made here.

NEED TO KNOW

MAP C3, D3

■ Enjoy a picnic in the mountains at one of the *cabildo* (local government) sites. Two of the best sites are Llanos de la Pez and Llanos de Ana López, both on the GC-600. You can also camp at a *cabildo*, as long as you obtain permission in advance from the local government (call 928 21 92 29 for further information).

Pretty Tejeda, set in the Caldera de Tejeda

7 Artenara

Cave culture rules in Gran Canaria's highest and chilliest town. Look around the simple 19th-century church, enjoy the fine views and pay a visit to the cave-chapel before a warming lunch.

8 Medicinal Plants Centre

For centuries, locals have relied on plants and natural remedies to cure illness and maintain health. This garden explains the medicinal uses and properties of hundreds of plants, herbs and flowers.

6 Cruz de Tejeda

All roads lead to Cruz de Tejeda, the large stone cross at the island's central point. Here you will find donkey rides, two superb restaurants, and a splendid Parador.

EXPLOSION AND EROSION

The rugged landscape of central Gran Canaria was not created overnight. Millions of years of explosive eruptions and steady erosion gave rise to the awe-inspiring Caldera de Tejeda. It's one of the oldest parts of the island; volcanic activity was at its height here around 10 million years ago. After a particularly violent explosion, the centre of the volcano sank, leaving a crater 18 km (11 miles) wide. The emblematic rocks crowning the crater are the result of five million years of erosion.

10 Mirador Degollada de la Becerra

Views don't get any better – from here you can see Roque Nublo, Roque Bentayga and, on clear days, Spain's highest peak, Mount Teide on Tenerife.

9 Museo de las Tradiciones

Housed in a restored, traditional rural house with a wooden balcony, this small museum recounts Tejeda's history, concentrating on the traditional crafts practised by villagers and including a re-creation of an old oil and vinegar shop.

Map of Tejeda

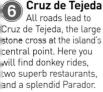

TOP 10 ⭐ Puerto de Mogán

Remote and hemmed in by mountains, this is Gran Canaria's most picturesque resort. It also claims to have the best climate in the world, enjoying more sunshine hours than Playa del Inglés and Maspalomas, and it has wonderful sunsets. Originally a small fishing village, Puerto de Mogán expanded to become a marina and resort, as land was reclaimed from the sea. It is because of the sea-filled channels beneath the houses and between the port and the beach that the resort is dubbed Little Venice.

1 Marina
A stopping-off point for ocean yachts crossing the Atlantic to the Caribbean, the marina **(above)** provides every facility for yacht owners, and it also offers a range of excursions and charter boats.

2 Cañada de los Gatos
This archaeological park, built more than a thousand years ago, includes a Guanche burial site. Adults are charged an admission fee of €4.

3 Diving
With sea temperatures that rarely fall below 20° C (68° F), a fishing-boat wreck lying at 20 m (66 ft) and an old stone pier, there's plenty to entice divers here. Expect to see parrotfish, morays and barracudas.

4 Los Azulejos
On the GC-200 road beyond Veneguera is a rock face of intense colours **(below)**. It was formed over millennia, as volcanic gases and fluids reacted with chemicals in the rocks.

5 Old Village
The houses clinging to the cliff face beyond Explanade de Castillete are the original fishing village **(above)**. They were all that existed here before land was reclaimed from the sea to construct the marina.

Municipal Street Market 6

The large, open-air, Friday market **(right)** is one of the busiest on the island. You'll find everything from fake designer labels to African carvings. It's a fabulous place to barter for bargains, but be wary of pickpockets.

7 Ermita de San Fernando

Constructed in 1935 by a local family, this simple chapel is where the wives of the fishermen came to pray for the safe return of their husbands, brothers and sons. Mass is said in English.

8 Whale and Dolphin Tours

Take a trip to see some of the 29 species of cetaceans that occupy the warm coastal waters, including bottlenose dolphins and short-finned pilot whales. Boats are monitored to comply with regulations.

FISHY PRACTICES

During the 19th century the fishermen of Puerto de Mogán would watch from their cave homes at the mouth of the ravine for shoals of tuna before setting sail from the small pebble beach. In 1911, a salting factory was constructed in the village, propelling the fishing industry into an economic boom and leading the way for expansion from small-scale production to major commercial activity. Fishing remains an important part of the economy today, and Puerto de Mogán is a popular destination for big-game fishers.

9 Craft Shops

Avoid the Friday market crowds and stroll the bougainvillea-lined cobbled streets behind the marina and beach, where, among the nautical suppliers, you'll find independent shops selling handmade candles, jewellery, clothing, souvenirs and leather goods.

NEED TO KNOW

MAP B5

Spirit of the Sea: whale- & dolphin-watching trips from Puerto Rico (pick-up from Puerto de Mogán). www.dolphin whale.co.uk. Adm: adults €27; children (3–12yrs) €14

Municipal Street Market: 8am–2pm Fri

Gran Canaria Divers: www.grancanaria divers.com. Single dives from €40, courses from €85

....

■ Try restaurant Playa de Mogán (Callejón Explanada del Castillete 8) for excellent fish.

10 Playa de Mogán

The sheltered, golden bay was constructed using sand imported from the Sahara. Gently sloping and with calm seas, it's a good beach for families and for snorkelling.

TOP 10 ⭐ Barranco de Guayadeque

Deep ravines are characteristic of Gran Canaria, but none of them is more impressive than the Barranco de Guayadeque (which in the Guanche language means "place of running water"). In addition to its great natural beauty, this fascinating area has an important cultural heritage, and harbours unique flora and fauna. The small local troglodyte population dwells in cave homes and strives to maintain a way of life that has been lost elsewhere on the island.

1 Flora and Fauna

Among 80 species of flora, there are two plants found nowhere else in the world. You might spot the island's only native mammal, a species of bat.

4 Guanche Settlements

Densely inhabited before the Conquest (see p38), the Barranco de Guayadeque is littered with caves, both natural and man-made. The finest is Cuevas Muchas.

2 Museo de Guayadeque

Based in a cave, this museum (above) offers an insight into life in the ravine, past and present. There is information on mummification, farming, the rare flora to be found here, and even how to build a cave home.

5 Ermita de San Bartolomé de Guayadeque

Nearly everything in Guayadeque's cave chapel, situated in Cuevas Bermejas, is carved out of the rock. When the hermitage was set up is not known, but the crucifix appears to date from just after the Conquest.

3 Almond Blossom

One of the best times to visit the Barranco de Guayadeque is in late January and early February, when the almond trees clinging to the sides of the ravine burst into a riot of pale pink and white blossom.

6 Views

The lookout point situated in Montaña de las Tierras provides a good view of the lower part of the ravine, though the best vistas are along GC-120 from Ingenio to Cuevas Blancas.

7 Troglodyte Village (Cuevas Bermejas)

Though the tradition of setting up home in a cave has survived, these 21st-century troglodyte abodes have little to do with their pre-Conquest counterparts. A peek through an open door is likely to reveal a television and even a fitted kitchen.

8 Cave Restaurants

Hearty traditional Canarian dishes, such as vegetable stew, goat and gofio (see p63), are on the menu at most of the local restaurants **(left)**, although the real appeal is the setting, not the cuisine.

A LANGUAGE LOST

Little has survived of the Guanche language – a mere smattering of words such as *baifo* (goat kid meat) and *gofio* (roasted corn or barley). You may, however, notice the many unusual place names on the island, most with a distinctly non-Spanish sound. Artenara, Agaete, Tocodoman and Tenteniguada are among the multitude of names whose origins predate the Conquest. Unfortunately, most of their meanings are lost; one of the few exceptions is Guayadeque.

9 Hiking

Hikers rule in the upper section of the ravine **(below)**, where the road fizzles out. The finest of several short walks skirts the Caldera de los Marteles.

View across the Barranco de Guayadeque

10 Montaña de las Tierras

The road comes to an abrupt halt at this small farming village. Follow the cobbled path from here for a tour of rural Gran Canaria. Four-wheel-drive vehicles can continue along the dirt track, but it's too rough for normal cars.

NEED TO KNOW

MAP E4 ■ GC-103 from Agüimes or GC-122 from Ingenio

Museo de Guayadeque: Carretera del Barranco de Guayadeque. 928 17 20 26. 9am–5pm Tue–Sat, 10am–3pm Sun. Adm: adults €2.50; children under 12 €1

■ Hike through the ravine, lying between Agüimes and Ingenio, to one of the most beautiful hamlets in the area, La Pasadilla. The yellow loquat trees here begin blossoming in autumn, and the fruits they produce can be found in local greengrocers' shops through spring and summer.

TOP 10 ⭐ Puerto de las Nieves

Puerto de las Nieves was once the island's principal port, but it suffered a blow in the 19th century with the construction of Puerto de la Luz in Las Palmas. The lack of major maritime traffic has allowed the enchanting harbour, with its blue-and-white houses, to retain its charm. Today it is the main departure point for Tenerife. Hundreds of visitors pass through the village everyday, but it merits more than a cursory glance through the bus window en route to the ferry.

1 Old Relics

Puerto de las Nieves seems to be a magnet for disused devices from long-gone glory days. The odd-looking 19th-century windmill in Avenida de los Poetas is the only one of its kind on the island, while the old jib crane and limekiln now serve to fill tourists' photograph albums.

2 Bajada de la Rama

This 4 August celebration (below) has its origins in a Guanche rain-making ceremony. Revellers gather here as much for the street party as for the tradition of beating the ocean with pine branches.

3 Fishing

If eating other people's catch isn't enough, you could join the locals on the wharf (below) and try to fish for your own. Or you could simply sip a coffee and watch the local fishermen repairing their nets in the harbour.

Harbour in Puerto de las Nieves

4 Reproduction of Maipés de Abajo

The Guanche burial site at this location was destroyed by construction work, and only a small reproduction of the tombs can be viewed here today. In contrast however, the Maipés de Arriba (see p43), in the Agaete Valley, survived the development of that area.

(see p43)

NEED TO KNOW

MAP B2

Ermita de las Nieves:
928 89 82 62.
11am–1pm Mon–Sat,
9–11am Sun

■ Sample the local brew: strong coffee grown in the Agaete valley.

■ Try to visit mid-week, as it gets very busy during weekends.

5 Seafood Restaurants

Sample the catch of the day in one of many family-run restaurants on the seafront **(above)**. If you can't decide on a dish, order a *parrillada* (mixed grill) of fish and seafood.

8 Dedo de Dios

The curious basaltic monolith known as the "Finger of God" was destroyed in 2005 by a tropical storm. Despite the fact that it no longer exists, it is still the emblem of the village.

9 Diving and Surfing

If the pace of the village is a little slow, try out local watersports. Scuba diving is popular around the cliffs near Dedo de Dios, while surfers prefer Punta de las Viejas, just north of the port.

6 Beach

Of the two beaches, most people opt for the one further from the port. There's no golden sand, but the calm, clean waters make up for the pebbles **(right)**.

7 Ferries to Tenerife

Boat trips to Tenerife leave from the port between 6:30am and 8:30pm and reach Santa Cruz in just over an hour.

10 Ermita de las Nieves

Model boats, gifts from fishermen, adorn the interior of this church. A Flemish triptych dedicated to the Virgen de las Nieves dominates.

The Top 10
of Everything

**Cenobio de Valerón – Guanche
artificial caves built to store grain**

🔟 Moments in History

① Volcanic Origins

Like all of the Canary Islands, Gran Canaria is volcanic in origin and first emerged from the ocean 15 million years ago. A second spurt of volcanic activity created the northeast of the island 11 million years later. Happily, the volcanoes have been extinct for 3,000 years.

Illustration of mummified Guanches

② Arrival of the First Inhabitants

It's generally agreed by historians that the Guanches were descended from the Berber tribes of Africa, but how they arrived in the Canary Islands is a mystery, as they did not have boat-building skills. The most plausible theory is that they arrived as slaves on Roman ships and then either escaped or were abandoned.

The 1599 Dutch assault

③ Early Exploration

Although Mallorcan friars had already successfully petitioned Rome to recognize Telde as the first Canarian municipality, it wasn't until 1405 that Jean de Béthencourt landed. Though he had taken Fuerteventura and Lanzarote, he could not overcome the tough Canarios. Juan Rejón had better luck in 1478, when he managed to set up the hamlet Real de Las Palmas, the island's future capital.

④ Baptism and Defeat

The indigenous Canarios proved no match for the Spanish invaders. The northern chief, Tenesor Semidan, was captured, baptized, and enlisted in the Spanish cause. Final defeat came in 1483, when many of the remaining fighters jumped into a deep ravine rather than live in slavery.

⑤ Pirates Attack

The archipelago's strategic position on the major trade routes brought fortune, but also trouble in the form of pirates. The defensive wall surrounding Las Palmas did little to protect it when Sir Francis Drake attacked in 1595, though he failed to defeat the locals. A more successful, 10-day assault by

Wartime shipping in the 1940s at Puerto de la Luz, the islands' principal port

Dutch corsair Pieter van der Does devastated the capital in 1599. Scores of churches and other historical buildings were sacked and burnt during the attacks.

6 Mass Emigration

Following Columbus's discovery of the New World, thousands of islanders headed across the ocean, settling throughout the Americas from Texas to Argentina. Most, however, made for the Caribbean islands and Venezuela. To this day, Venezuela is known as the "eighth island" because of its strong family links with the Canarian archipelago.

7 Boom and Bust

Contact with Latin America led to fierce competition, and Gran Canaria's sugar cane industry was ruined by tumbling prices. The wine and cochineal (food colouring) trades went the same way, and, by the end of the 19th century, things were looking desperate, rekindling the mass exodus to Latin America.

8 Getting Connected

The development of Puerto de la Luz in 1881 was to change the island's fortunes forever. It soon became the archipelago's principal port and today it is one of Europe's largest. The Canary Islands' first airport was built halfway down Gran Canaria's east coast in 1930.

9 Franco Launches his Military Coup

When Spanish officials got wind of a rebellious general in March 1936, they quickly shipped him off to the Canary Islands. However, in July, General Francisco Franco and his followers launched an uprising from their headquarters in Las Palmas. It was the beginning of the Spanish Civil War. In 1939, Franco came to power and established Fascist rule.

General Franco in Las Palmas

10 Tourism Takes Hold

After the failed industries of earlier centuries, the islands needed a more stable source of income. Salvation arrived in the 1960s in the form of mass construction, and tomato plantations were soon giving way to hotels. Tourism is now the pillar of the islands' economy. Rather than somewhere to escape from, Gran Canaria has now become a favoured destination for visitors.

🔟 Historical Buildings

1 Teatro Pérez Galdós, Las Palmas

MAP M5 ▪ Plaza de Stagno 1
▪ www.teatroperezgaldos.es

Little remains of the original 19th-century structure, almost completely destroyed by fire. Today's theatre is the result of a restoration project by architects Marcos Roger Berghänel and Carlos Díaz.

Teatro Pérez Galdós, Las Palmas

2 Castillo de la Luz

The island's oldest and best example of military architecture dates from the 15th century; it was severely damaged in 1599 by Dutch pirates and has been extensively restored since.

3 Heredad de Aguas, Arucas

MAP D2 ▪ C/La Heredad 1

Without their sophisticated irrigation system, the inhabitants of Arucas would not have enjoyed the prosperity they did during the sugar cane years. These days bananas are the main crop, but the water channels are no less important, so it's fitting that the water board should have such grand headquarters. Completed in the early 20th century, the building is topped by an elegant dome.

4 Finca Condal, Juan Grande

MAP E5 ▪ GC-500

There's no denying the splendour of the Count of Vega Grande's former home, now a popular events venue. Dating back to the 16th century, the low, whitewashed house is topped by a red-tiled roof. Next door there is a church, which was built around the same time and has been restored it to its former glory in renovations.

5 Windmills, La Aldea de San Nicolás

MAP B3

On the road from the old town to the coast, there are two fine windmills, built in the 19th century and now restored. The watermill on the road to Artenara is still in working order and has become a delightful *casa rural*.

6 Casa de Colón, Las Palmas

Although heavily restored, this exquisite building reveals traces of its 15th-century roots. Together with several other adjoining houses, this is now the home of the Christopher Columbus museum *(see pp12–13)*.

Casa de Colón, Las Palmas

7 Casa de los Quintana, Santa María de Guía

MAP C1 ■ Plaza Mayor de Guía

Only the presence of a goat and a plate of *gofio* could make this house look more Canarian. A small dragon tree stands by the entrance to the picturesque 17th-century structure, with its superlative balcony. Home of the town's first mayor, it bears his family coat of arms.

8 Casa de los Patronos de la Virgen, Teror

A pristine example of Canarian architecture, complete with an interior patio and rickety-looking wooden balconies *(see p25)*.

9 Cuartel de El Colmenar, Valsequillo

MAP E3 ■ Colmenar Bajo

Originally a cavalry barracks, this fine example of Canarian architecture, built in 1530, is a contender for the title of Gran Canaria's oldest building.

Gabinete Literario, Las Palmas

10 Gabinete Literario, Las Palmas

MAP L5 ■ Plaza de Cairasco

The grand façade is striking, but you have to step inside this Modernist masterpiece to fully appreciate its splendour. The interior is lavishly decked out in fine Renaissance style, setting it apart from other buildings in the capital. Once the location of the city's first theatre, it is now home to a cultural centre.

TOP 10 MODERN BUILDINGS

Auditorio Alfredo Kraus

1 Auditorio Alfredo Kraus, Las Palmas
Oscar Tusquets' beachfront masterpiece *(see p75)*.

2 Palacio de Congresos, Maspalomas
MAP D6 ■ Plaza de las Convenciones
This circular glass edifice is an important conference centre.

3 Iglesia del Sagrado Corazón de Jesus, Balos
MAP E4
A church with an asymmetrical roof and monochrome stained glass.

4 Police Station, Las Palmas
MAP J4 ■ C/Alcalde Bethencourt
Locals either love or loathe this multicoloured tower.

5 El Muelle, Las Palmas
An award-winning Modernist mall opened in 2003 *(see p77)*.

6 AC Hotel, Las Palmas
MAP P2 ■ C/Eduardo Benot 3
By night, lights illuminate this grand 13-storey, cylindrical hotel.

7 Urbanización Turística, Puerto de Mogán
MAP B5
A striking, white bougainvillea-draped tourist complex.

8 Gobierno de Canarias, Las Palmas
MAP H3 ■ C/León y Castillo 57
This pleasing government structure fits in well with its surroundings.

9 Biblioteca Pública del Estado, Las Palmas
MAP K5 ■ Avda Marítima
Agreeably asymmetrical, this huge library was built in 2002.

10 Cabildo Insular, Las Palmas
MAP L4 ■ C/Bravo Murillo
The island's finest example of Spanish rationalist architecture.

TOP 10 Guanche Sites

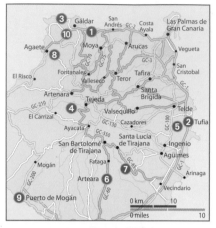

inhabited by Guanches now house 21st-century troglodytes, but the stone constructions are still in their original state. Dominating the scene is an immense *tagoror* (stone circle), where the elders would meet to make important decisions *(see p96)*.

3 Túmulo de La Guancha

Though rather average when compared to the tombs of Egyptian royalty, this Guanche cemetery outshines others scattered around the island. It's thought that the central sepulchre contained the *guanarteme* (king), while the aristocracy were laid to rest around him *(see p84)*.

4 Roque Bentayga

Numerous dwellings and grain stores have been unearthed around this huge monolith, the remnant of a volcanic crater, which was considered sacred by the Guanches *(see p28 & p87)*.

The tiny caves of Cenobio de Valerón

1 Cenobio de Valerón

Built without the use of modern tools, this cluster of miniature artificial caves represents an awe-inspiring feat of early engineering. For years, experts believed it to be a convent, but it is now widely agreed that the caves were used to store grain *(see p82)*.

2 Tufia

This settlement is unusual as it has examples of both types of aboriginal home common to the island: cave dwellings, and the low stone houses unique to Gran Canaria. The coastal caves once

Roque Bentayga

The atmospheric Cuatro Puertas

⑤ Cuatro Puertas

If other aboriginal sites on the island fail to impress, visit Cuatro Puertas. This is the most remarkable man-made cave on Gran Canaria and in the whole archipelago. The large room with four "doors" was once a sacred place. A clear path marks the route around the site *(see p97)*.

⑥ Arteara

The island's most important Guanche burial site is in an impressive location, nestled in a palm grove in the Fataga ravine. Making out the circular tombs among the debris of a stark lava field is not easy, but information panels help you to differentiate the sepulchres from the other rocks. The site covers an area 2 km (1 mile) wide *(see p101)*.

⑦ La Fortaleza de Ansite
MAP D4

The Guanches' last stronghold is pitted with caves overlooking the Tirajana ravine. You can imagine the islanders' terrible plight as they tried to repel the Spaniards, then threw themselves into the ravine shouting the patriotic motto *"Atis Tirma"* (For My Land).

⑧ Maipés de Arriba
MAP C2

Featuring around 500 tombs, the Maipés de Arriba may have been the principal burial ground for lowly Guanches. Look out for the different styles of tomb, particularly the circular towers, which were almost certainly the last resting place of aboriginal aristocracy. A similar site closer to the coast, the Maipés de Abajo, was destroyed by modern development; there's a small-scale reproduction of it in Puerto de las Nieves *(see p34)*.

⑨ Cañada de los Gatos
MAP B5 ■ C/La Puntilla ■ 638 81 06 21. Open Tue–Sun 10am–5pm (6pm in summer) ■ Adm

At this recently excavated coastal settlement at the mouth of the Mogán ravine, pathways lead around the well-preserved remains of 1,300-year-old houses, burial pits and caves. There's also a café on site.

Paintings in Cueva Pintada

⑩ Cueva Pintada

In 1860, a local farmer stumbled across this painted cave, uncovering probably the most important archaeological find – and certainly the finest set of aboriginal paintings – in the whole archipelago. In 2006, after more than 20 years of repairs, the Cueva Pintada reopened to the public. The 3D film transports you back in time to the beginning of the Spanish conquest *(see p81)*.

TOP 10 Museums

Display in Museo Elder de la Ciencia y la Tecnología, Las Palmas

1 Museo Elder de la Ciencia y la Tecnología, Las Palmas

The capital's science museum offers a perfect blend of education and entertainment, with plenty of interactive exhibits to keep visitors of all ages amused (see p73).

2 Casa de Colón, Las Palmas

Take a fascinating journey through the history of navigation and the discovery of America in the lovely setting of one of the island's most attractive buildings (see pp12–13).

3 Museo de Guayadeque

Cave living, past and present, gets its own absorbing museum in a spectacular ravine setting. There are some fascinating archaeological finds on display (see p32).

4 Museo de Historia de Agüimes

MAP E4 ▪ C/Juan Alvarado y Saz 42 ▪ 928 78 54 53 ▪ Open 9am–5pm Tue–Sun ▪ Adm ▪ No disabled access

Inhabited since Guanche times, Agüimes has a full and interesting past that warrants a museum in its honour. Visitors can learn about the area's many ancient legends and superstitions, a product of its great ethnic mix. Displayed in a handsome 17th-century mansion, the exhibits are well laid out, and information is provided in three languages.

5 Casa-Museo Antonio Padrón, Gáldar

Many of Antonio Padrón's colourful paintings portray Canarian customs and daily life, though the collection here does include a number of his Expressionist works. The museum is set on the main pedestrianized street in his home town (see p80).

6 Casa de los Patronos de la Virgen, Teror

The patrons of Gran Canaria's most important statue of the Virgin resided for centuries in this sparkling example of Canarian architecture. Today it is preserved as a museum, complete with period furniture and paintings (see p25).

Exhibit in Casa de Colón, Las Palmas

7 Museo Canario, Las Palmas

A mesmerizing peek into the life of the Guanches, Gran Canaria's enigmatic pre-Hispanic inhabitants, is provided here. There are some superb exhibits unearthed from around the island (see pp16–17).

8 Museo Néstor, Las Palmas

Admire the finest works of Gran Canarian Modernist maestro Néstor Martín Fernández de la Torre in the Pueblo Canario, designed and built in the 1930s by the artist's brother Miguel. One of the museum's highlights, the eight-panel *Poema del Atlántico* is widely considered to be the artist's finest work, though the sensitivity shown in *Poema de la Tierra* is also remarkable (see p74).

Painting in Museo Néstor, Las Palmas

9 Ecomuseo Casa-Alfar Panchito, La Atalaya

MAP E3 ■ Camino de la Picota 11 ■ **928 28 82 70** ■ Open 10am–2pm daily ■ Adm

Visit the former cave home and workshop of a master of traditional Guanche pottery, and see a side of Canarian life that is all but lost.

10 CAAM, Las Palmas

Set in the historic quarter of Las Palmas is this ultra-modern art gallery, which mounts temporary exhibitions by Spanish, African and Latin-American artists (see p76).

TOP 10 MUSEUM EXHIBITS

1 Poema del Atlántico, Museo Néstor
Néstor's magnum opus shows the ocean at different times of day.

2 Drawing Room, Casa de los Patronos de la Virgen
This room contains some fine antique furniture and portraits.

3 Piedad, Casa Museo Antonio Padrón
Antonio Padrón's final painting – he died before completing it.

4 Foucault's Pendulum, Museo Elder de la Ciencia y la Tecnología
Watch this massive pendulum gradually knocking over small posts, proving that the earth rotates.

5 Idolo de Tara, Museo Canario
This terracotta figure, thought to be a fertility symbol, is the island's largest and most important pre-Hispanic idol.

6 Poema de la Tierra, Museo Néstor
This reflective work depicts the seasons and the times of day.

7 Astrolabe, Casa de Colón
This 15th-century metal navigational device is one of a kind.

8 Watermill, Museo de Guayadeque
An interactive model explains the workings of a watermill.

9 Superstitions and Witchcraft, Museo de Historia de Agüimes
Spinning panels relate the surprising beliefs of early settlers.

10 Workshop, Ecomuseo Casa-Alfar Panchito
Gain an insight into Guanche pottery at this ceramics maestro's workshop.

***Poema de la Tierra*, Museo Néstor**

🔟 Churches

Templo Parroquial de San Sebastián

1 Templo Parroquial de San Sebastián, Agüimes

MAP E4 ▪ Plaza Nuestra Señora del Rosario

Follow the maze of cobbled alleys in Agüimes and eventually you'll reach the magnificent Templo Parroquial de San Sebastián. A supreme example of Canarian Neo-Classical architecture, it has the air of a cathedral rather than a church. Although started in 1796, the church was not completed until 1940.

2 Iglesia de Nuestra Señora de la Concepción, Agaete

MAP C2 ▪ C/Juan Valls y Roca 1

The bright red dome crowning Agaete's church sets it apart from other churches built in a similar Neo-Classical style.

3 Catedral de Santa Ana, Las Palmas

Extending across 7,000 sq m (75,350 sq ft), the capital's cathedral is an impressive blend of architectural styles. Some important Luján Pérez sculptures and remnants of the original Gothic structure can be seen inside (see pp14–15).

4 Basílica de San Juan Bautista, Telde

The façade of Telde's main church is as forbidding as its heavy wooden door, evoking thoughts of medieval castles. Inside, a Flemish altarpiece, among the most precious works of art in the Canary Islands, outshines the main Baroque altarpiece. The figure of Christ was modelled from corn paste by Michoacan Mexicans in 1550 (see p98).

5 Iglesia de la Candelaria, Ingenio

MAP E4 ▪ C/Hermanos Fullana 5

This 20th-century church features sculptures of San José and San Blás by Luján Pérez (see p15).

6 Basílica de Nuestra Señora del Pino, Teror

Rebuilt and renovated countless times, this immense basilica draws many pilgrims (see pp26–7).

Lofty interior of Basílica de Nuestra Señora del Pino, Teror

7 Parroquia de Nuestra Señora de la Candelaria, Moya

This large 20th-century church, with twin bell towers, is the focal point of sleepy Moya, but its most memorable feature is its vertiginous location, perched precariously atop a rugged ravine *(see p82)*.

Parroquia de San Juan Bautista

8 Parroquia de San Juan Bautista, Arucas

Behind the ornate façade of the island's most striking church, built largely from volcanic rock, lies an equally impressive interior full of sculptures, stained-glass windows and a grand altarpiece *(see p82)*.

9 Iglesia de Santa Lucía, Santa Lucía de Tirajana

MAP D4 ▪ Plaza de Santa Lucía

Built in 1905, this pretty church looks rather like a mosque, owing to its pronounced dome.

10 Iglesia de Santiago de los Caballeros, Gáldar

MAP C1 ▪ Plaza de Santiago

Unusually, this church was built in a blend of Baroque and Neo-Classical styles. Check out the *pila verde* (green font), allegedly where Canarians were baptized when the Spanish first took over.

TOP 10 ERMITAS

Ermita de la Virgen de la Cuevita

1 Ermita de la Virgen de la Cuevita, Artenara
The patron saint of cyclists resides in this small rock-face chapel *(see p87)*.

2 Ermita de las Nieves, Puerto de las Nieves
This church started out as a shrine in a 15th-century fortified tower *(see p35)*.

3 Ermita de San Antonio Abad, Las Palmas
Columbus is said to have prayed here before his trip to the New World *(see p13)*.

4 Ermita de la Inmaculada Concepción, La Atalaya
MAP E3 ▪ Calle La Concepción
This simple 18th-century church resembles a rural house.

5 Ermita de San Telmo, Las Palmas
Rebuilt in 1694, the original church was destroyed by Dutch pirates *(see p76)*.

6 Ermita de San Isidro, San Isidro
MAP D3
Forebears of the current owners built this pleasing 17th-century church.

7 Ermita de San Sebastián, Agaete
MAP C2 ▪ Calle Pescadores
This *mudéjar*-style hermitage has an elaborate ceiling.

8 Ermita de San Isidro el Viejo, Gáldar
MAP C1 ▪ Carretera de Caideros
This mosque-like building is perhaps the island's smallest place of worship.

9 Ermita de San Roque, Valsequillo
MAP E3 ▪ Plaza de San Roque
This 20th-century church is backed by an impressive palm grove.

10 Ermita de Ayacata, Ayacata (near Vecindario)
MAP E5
In February, this church is completely enveloped in almond blossom.

🔟 Beauty Spots

① Montañón Negro
MAP C3

Canarian pine stands out against the stark black landscape of Gran Canaria's most recent, yet long-extinct, volcano. Its last eruption some 3,000 years ago left a deep and arresting crater, the Caldera de los Pinos de Gáldar.

Los Azulejos – multicoloured cliffs

② Los Azulejos
MAP B4

As you reach Mogán from La Aldea de San Nicolás, the sparse cliffs suddenly light up with a rainbow of colours, ranging from blue to brown and passing through every shade of green and yellow. In winter, small waterfalls trickle down the cliffs, further enhancing their beauty.

③ Dunas de Maspalomas
If you're feeling energetic, take the tough trek through these magnificent, golden, shifting sand dunes to the point where the hotels peter out and nothing but sand can be seen (see pp20–21).

④ Los Tilos de Moya
Outside of the Botanical Garden, this is Gran Canaria's only area of *laurisilva* (see p19). Stroll through this lost world of vegetation, almost wiped out in Europe in the last ice age. Myrtle and heather flourish alongside the many laurel species (see p82).

⑤ Barranco de los Cernícalos
MAP E3

This ravine has year-round running water, a rarity on Gran Canaria. Admire the changing vegetation as you reach the highest waterfall on an easy walk that takes you through willow trees and olive groves. Look out for flora unique to the island, such as the vivid orange Canarian bellflower and Tenteniguada viper's bugloss, noted for its blue conical flowers. Access is via Lomo Magullo.

⑥ Barranco de Guayadeque
Fascinating flora, important heritage and an unusual way of life coexist in the most spectacular of Gran Canaria's ravines (see pp32–3).

⑦ Parque Natural de Pilancones
MAP C4–5 & D4–5

Though not as lush or as dense as its northern counterpart, Tamadaba, Pilancones is still impressive. Almost 5,800 ha (14,332 acres) of Canarian pine forest, it's an unrivalled place for bird-watching. Look out for the great spotted woodpecker.

The impressive Dunas de Maspalomas

The stunning Presa de las Niñas

8 Presa de las Niñas

The island's most attractive reservoir is also its most popular. On weekends, especially, you will have to share its beauty with more than a few picnickers. In the week, however, it's less busy, and you can enjoy a peaceful stroll in the small pine wood and imagine perhaps that you are in Canada rather than the Canaries. There is also a well-equipped picnic area and camp site here, though you will need a permit from the *cabildo* (council) to make use of the latter *(see pp102–3)*.

9 Pinar de Tamadaba

Enjoy the view from this peaceful spot, rich in Canarian pine and home to some incredibly rare endemic flowers, found only in this corner of the island. In the Guanche language, Tamadaba meant "hollow", though much of the forest is in fact higher than the surrounding land *(see p89)*.

10 Jardín Botánico Viera y Clavijo

Enjoy the riches of Canarian flora in this perfectly laid-out garden, an easy day trip from the capital, Las Palmas. As well as native plants, there's a variety of tropical and imported species that thrive in the island's mild climate *(see pp18–19)*.

🔟 Beaches

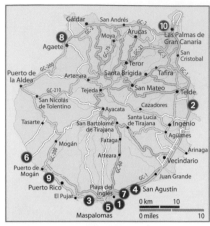

opportunities. Though easy to reach, this east-coast beach is often deserted, as the majority of holidaymakers prefer the guaranteed good weather further south. Watch the planes take off and land at the nearby airport, or contemplate the aboriginal ruins at Tufia (see p96).

3 Montaña Arena
MAP C6

Untouched by the swathe of development that plagues the south coast, this stretch of dark sand has no amenities. Favoured by nudists, it is away from the crowds without being too far from civilization. To get there, park at the camp site west of Pasito Blanco, head for the stony beach and take a vertiginous path to the left.

4 San Agustín
MAP F4

Most of the bathers here are Canarian daytrippers from the capital, but some tourists are getting wise to this gem. Calm waters border the black-sand beach, split into three sections by rocky outcrops.

Playa del Inglés is popular with tourists

1 Playa del Inglés
MAP D6

Maspalomas's closest neighbour is one of the island's busiest beaches, but it's large enough for all to enjoy its fine golden sand. For those who like a few amenities while they bathe, there's no lack of bars or sunloungers and, as you'd expect, the resort here is well served with restaurants and hotels (see p105 and pp113–15).

2 Aguadulce
MAP F3

Below the Guanche settlement of Tufia lies a quiet, sheltered cove with 140 m (459 ft) of golden sand, and good snorkelling and diving

The black sands of San Agustín

The beach at Maspalomas, with a backdrop of spectacular sand dunes

5 Maspalomas

Although it's one of the islands' largest resorts, this is an unrivalled place to sunbathe, bordered by the dazzling sand dunes (see pp20–21).

6 Veneguera
MAP B5

This is another pristine beach favoured by nudists. After Veneguera village the roads are only passable with a four-wheel drive. Those in other vehicles can park and walk the last section. Backed by towering cliffs, the black sand and pebbles are lapped by a calm stretch of ocean.

7 Las Burras
MAP D6

If you don't mind a bit of wind, Las Burras makes a good alternative to the busier resort beaches further along the coast. A favourite with locals, the calm waters are perfect for those with children.

8 El Juncal
MAP B2

Few sun-seekers venture to this secluded cove, but those who do are rewarded with exceptionally calm waters surrounded by stunning cliffs. From the GC-2 heading west, take the exit after km 29, then keep heading left through the tomato plantations. Once you reach a plain, park and walk the last 20 minutes down the ravine that gives the beach its name.

9 Amadores
MAP B5

Located in the sunniest part of the island, Amadores offers a crescent of golden sand with plentiful facilities, such as windsurfing, diving and boat excursions, as well as a large number of restaurants and bars. The fabulous cliff walk between Amadores and nearby Puerto Rico gives superb views of the beach.

Crescent-shaped bay at Amadores

10 Las Canteras
Map N2

Swim with the fish in the crystalline waters of the capital's 2.8-km (1.7-mile) golden beach. A rocky reef keeps the waves back, making this a superb place for families to swim. Further south, the reef ends and surfers take advantage of the breaks. If you prefer to stay dry, take a gentle stroll along the promenade, stopping in La Puntilla for a seafood lunch.

🔟 Marine Activities

Windsurfers enjoy riding the waves in Pozo Izquierdo

1 Surfing
PRO Surfing: 628 10 40 25; www.prsurfing.com

Few European destinations offer such good surf as Gran Canaria, a fact made clear by the number of blond-streaked enthusiasts in search of the perfect wave. Schools operate across the island, although the rougher northern coast has more appeal for experts.

2 Diving
Sunsub: 928 77 81 65; www.sunsub.com ■ 7 Mares: 928 46 00 35; www.7mares.es

Whether your interest is marine life or sunken ships, diving in the seas off Gran Canaria is a satisfying affair.

Diving off the coast of Gran Canaria

Marine species from Europe, Africa and even the Caribbean mingle here, and the high number of shipwrecks adds extra interest. Playa del Cabrón, Pasito Blanco and Sardina del Norte all offer superlative dives, while the bulk of the wrecks are off the coast of Las Palmas.

3 Swimming
Canarian waters are blessed with a lack of anything that bites. On the other hand, do not expect warm seas, as this is the Atlantic. The south and east coasts are generally safe, though currents and strong waves plague the north and west. If you fancy a dip in the north, head for one of the natural pools (see p84).

4 Windsurfing
Centro Internacional de Windsurfing: 928 12 14 00; www. pozo-ciw.com

Pozo Izquierdo plays host to an international competition in the summer, though its waters are not suited for novices. The school here takes those starting out in the sport to calmer seas until they are up to windsurfing with the experts.

5 Stand Up Paddle Boarding
Las Alcaravaneras and Las Canteras are great beaches to try stand up paddle boarding. You can also try it at night through Mojosurf at the latter.

6 Snorkelling

Gran Canaria is superb for snorkelling. There's no need to stray further than the capital's beach, Las Canteras, for encounters with parrotfish, octopus, ornate wrasse and countless species of sea bream.

7 Fishing

Dorado: 664 089 50 ■ www.marlincanariasportfishing.com

Gran Canaria has fishing aplenty. The best deep-sea trips are out of Puerto Rico, where tuna, marlin and swordfish abound in summer.

8 Boat Trips

Charter a luxury yacht, gaze down into the ocean from a glass-bottomed boat, or live it up on a booze cruise. Puerto Rico is the best place from which to set sail, but there are also trips from Las Palmas and Playa del Inglés.

Sailing boats in Puerto de Mogán

9 Sailing

Atlantic Islands Sail Training Centre: 928 56 59 31; www.aistrac.com

Whether you want to hire a boat and go it alone, or learn how to sail, Gran Canaria offers plenty of possibilities. The season is from April to October, though enthusiasts can be catered for all year round.

10 Kayaking

Canariaventura: 928 76 61 68; www.canariaventura.com

There is no better way to appreciate the island's diverse coastline than from a kayak. Beginners can get started at Playa de las Canteras, while the more adventurous may like to join a tour of the southern coast.

TOP 10 UNDERWATER ENCOUNTERS

Parrotfish, a frequent sight

1 Parrotfish
Whether you're snorkelling or on a deep dive, you are almost guaranteed to see the island's most emblematic underwater creature.

2 Bluefin Damselfish
These fish are abundant, but you won't tire of seeing the vivid blue glint contrasted against the black scales.

3 Angel Shark
This is the most commonly sighted shark, often mistaken for a ray owing to its flat body.

4 Ornate Wrasse
The blue-green shimmer of the ornate wrasse is a familiar but pleasing sight on any dive from Gran Canaria.

5 Octopus
A creature that frequently lurks on the seabed, but can be seen from surface level down to 100 m (330 ft).

6 Spiny Butterfly Ray
This mottled fish, which measures up to 1.5 m (5 ft), often hides, unnoticed, in the sand.

7 Tiger Moray
One of a number of serpentine fish, the Tiger Moray is unmistakable, with its bright yellow skin and evil-looking, fang-like teeth.

8 Trumpetfish
A comical species that can change colour according to its mood. Frequently seen on deeper dives.

9 Scorpionfish
Numerous species of this spiky fish swim in the Canarian seas. They usually favour rocky areas.

10 Shipwrecks
Ships have been sinking off these shores ever since ports were built, so there are wrecks aplenty sprinkled around the coast.

🔟 Hiking

1 San Pedro to Tamadaba
MAP C2

Beginning in the village of San Pedro near the top of Agaete Valley, this 8-hour circular route climbs steeply into Tamadaba Park, passing abandoned cave houses in El Hornillo, to reach the splendid Peréz and Lugarejos reservoirs.

San Pedro to Tamadaba

2 Camino de la Plata
MAP D3

In the 19th century this route along the old *camino real* was improved to allow people and their donkeys to travel over the Highlands to Ayacata. Allow 2.5 hours.

3 Cruz de Tejeda to Artenara
MAP D3

This demanding, 8-hour circular route follows the Tejeda Barranco border with views over Roque Nublo and Roque Bentayga, and on a clear day, across to Mount Teide on Tenerife. The return is via Roque Bentayga.

4 Barranco de los Cernícalos
MAP E3

Take the road out of Lomo Magullo towards Los Arenales. A clear path leads you along the lush ravine, where a stream trickles throughout the year. As well as appealing to lovers of flora, the hike rewards all with its impressive finale: a series of ever-higher waterfalls. Allow about 3 hours for this out-and-back hiking trip.

5 Caldera de Bandama

Formed 2000 years ago, when a magma chamber collapsed in on itself, this classic circular walk, taking 1.5 hours, descends to the floor of the crater, covered in endemic flora *(see p95)*.

6 Santa Lucía de Tirajana to Fortaleza de Ansite
MAP D4

This 3-hour hike leads you through idyllic countryside to the Fortaleza de Ansite. Take the path leading from km 49 of the GC-65, then keep left at all forks. While here, visit the dazzling La Sorrueda reservoir.

7 Roque Nublo
MAP C3

This challenging circular route takes 7 hours and is considered one of the best walks on the island. It climbs from the mountain village of Tejeda to Roque Nublo before continuing to Roque Bentayga and descending back into Tejeda Valley.

Hikers descending from Roque Nublo

8 The Dam Circuit
MAP C4–D4

This breathtaking hike skirts three of the island's reservoirs. Starting from the GC-605 north of Presa de las Niñas, it hugs the Soria dam and passes north of Chira. The walk takes 7 hours and ends at Cruz Grande, but you could break for the night at Los Cercados.

Trail heading towards Chira

9 Cruz Grande
MAP D4

This easy route, taking 4.5 hours, starts and ends in Degollada de Cruz Grande and follows a path through the Parque Natural de Pilancones, an area rich in native orchids, lavender and Black Bugloss.

10 Around Chira
MAP C4

From the Degollada de Cruz Grande, this circular trail traverses a ridge to reach the lake at Chira. Crossing the lake dam, it returns via a series of viewpoints. Allow 2.5 hours.

TOP 10 HIKING TIPS

Hiking in Gran Canaria

1 It's always advisable to wear strong sun screen and a hat when hiking, whatever the time of year.

2 In the mountains, temperatures can be considerably cooler (and much hotter in summer) than on the coast. It's best to wear layers.

3 Make sure you carry sufficient water for everyone in the group; one litre per person is advised.

4 On long hikes, you should think about setting off early to avoid the worst heat of the day.

5 Check the weather forecast before you set off and don't go hiking if there is any kind of weather alert in place. The website www.aemet.es is the most reliable place to check.

6 It's not advisable to go walking in the mountains in July, August or September. The higher you get, the hotter it can become. Heat exhaustion is common at this time of year and deaths have been known.

7 Volcanic terrain can be really tough under foot; make sure you wear proper hiking boots with a good level of ankle support.

8 Hiking poles are a good idea to help cope with steep ascents and descents.

9 Mountain routes can be vertiginous; always check directions and heights before you set out.

10 Unless you're hiking to a known lunch spot, make sure you always take a packed lunch.

🔟 Drives and Cycle Routes

1 Agüimes to Maspalomas via Temisas, Santa Lucía de Tirajana and Fataga (drive)
MAP E4–D6

Break up this winding drive with stops at Temisas (see p96) and Fataga (see p100), and at the *mirador* (viewpoint) on the road to Maspalomas. A detour takes you to La Sorrueda reservoir and on to La Fortaleza de Ansite (see p43), south of Santa Lucía de Tirajana.

View on the Gáldar to Moya drive

2 Gáldar to Moya via Fontanales (drive)
MAP C1–D2

The GC-220 passes Hoya de Pineda, a troglodyte village, before reaching Pinos de Gáldar pine forest. Pause at the superb Mirador de Los Pinos de Gáldar before taking the GC-70 past Fontanales and then a scenic side road, the GC-700, on to Moya (see p82).

Los Azulejos, on the West Coast drive

3 Mogán to Pico de las Nieves (drive)
MAP B4–D3

After heavy rain, waterfalls appear along the winding road that leads to the island's highest point (see p28).

4 Tamadaba (drive)
MAP C3

The glorious views and lush scenery make this circular drive a favourite. Follow the GC-216 from Cruz de Acusa, near Artenara, and take the loop around Gran Canaria's finest pine forest. The road is one-way.

5 Maspalomas (cycle route)
MAP D6–5

A short but testing 26 km (16 miles) from Maspalomas, the GC-503 takes you north of the Aquapark. Following the GC-504, the road climbs up to the reservoir at Ayagaures before steeply ascending to Cima Pedro González and finally dropping back to the coast along the GC-503.

6 The West Coast (drive)
MAP C2–B4

Not for the faint-hearted, the road from Agaete (see p83) to Mogán (see p103) has stunning coastal views. Stop off in Playa de la Aldea for lunch, before turning inland. The village of Veneguera merits a stop, and look out for the cliffs of Los Azulejos (see p48).

7 Island Circuit (cycle route)
MAP B5

For those with the leg strength and the stamina, this 190-km (118-mile) circular route circumnavigates the island, beginning and ending in Puerto de Mogán. Riding entirely on paved surfaces, you tackle testing gradients into the mountains and Tamadaba (see p89), before skirting Las Palmas and following the coast south.

8 Teror to Artenara (drive)
MAP D2–C3

The highlights of this drive along the GC-21 are the stretch overlooking the Barranco de Valsendero and two stunning *miradors*, Balcón de Zamora and Los Pinos de Gáldar (see p89).

Part of the drive from Teror to Artenara

9 Mogán to Soria (cycle route)
MAP B4–C6

An arduous ride from Mogán through the Tauropass (see p102) is one of Spain's best climbs. From the beautiful Soria reservoir, the descent takes you down to Arguineguín (see p64) for the coastal ride back to Mogán. A breathtaking 68-km (42-mile) round trip.

10 Playa del Inglés to Santa Lucía de Tirajana (cycle route)
MAP D6–4

This 73-km (45-mile) route climbs from Playa del Inglés (see p50) through Sardina del Sur and the Las Carboneras mountains to reach Santa Lucía de Tirajana (see p103) and Tunte. The return descent through Fataga is a panoramic ride back to the coast.

TOP 10 MIRADORS

View from Degollada de la Becerra

1 Pico de Bandama
MAP E3
From the crater's peak, you can see the capital, coast and mountains.

2 Pico de las Nieves
Lucky visitors can see the coast from the island's highest point, but many get only mist (see p28).

3 Degollada de la Becerra
On a clear day, Mount Teide makes a fine backdrop to this already stunning view of Roque Bentayga, Tejeda and the Acusa flatlands (see p29).

4 Degollada de las Palomas
MAP D3
A window over the Tejeda ravine, this viewpoint is great for spotting hawks.

5 Mirador del Balcón, La Aldea de San Nicolás
After driving the white-knuckle west coast, catch your breath and admire the stunning sheer cliffs (see p90).

6 Mirador de la Montaña de Arucas
MAP D2
A viewpoint and restaurant with views over Las Palmas, Arucas and the ocean.

7 Barranco de Fataga
MAP D4
A *mirador* with a superb view over the Fataga ravine.

8 Cima Pedro González
MAP D4
The Ayagaures dam, with its pretty rural village, is visible at the end of the ravine.

9 Cruz Grande
Admire views over the Barranco de las Tederas and Pilancones forest (see p48).

10 Los Pinos de Gáldar
MAP C2
Look into the depths of the imposing crater, dotted with Canarian pine trees.

🔟 **Outdoor Activities**

Gran Canarian golf course with a view

1 Golf
Las Palmeras Golf: Avda Dr Alfonso Chiscano Díaz s/n; 928 22 23 33; www.laspalmerasgolf.es
Golfers are well catered for, with eight 18-hole courses, plus a few nine-hole pitch and putts. The mild climate has made golf a major draw. Most courses are in the south, though the Real Club de Golf (see p98) is just outside Las Palmas and the Las Palmeras Golf Sport Urban Resort is in Las Palmas itself.

2 Football
Estadio de Gran Canaria: MAP E2; C/ Fondos de Segura s/n, Las Palmas; 928 24 13 42; www.udlas palmas.es
Most Spaniards love the "beautiful game", and Canarians are no

A UD Las Palmas football game

exception. Even if you're not a football fan, watching a match can be a wonderful way to spend a Sunday afternoon and a good way to get to know the locals. Gran Canaria's biggest team, UD Las Palmas, play in La Liga (the Spanish Premier League) against major Spanish football clubs such as Atlético Madrid, Real Madrid and Barcelona.

3 Climbing
Climbo: MAP C3; 636 89 84 93; www.climborocks.com
Gran Canaria's volcanic terrain – in particular the central peaks – is simply a dream for climbers. Roque Nublo alone has 12 routes, while Ayacata is another top spot more suited to beginners.

4 Parapente
Club Siroco: 606 42 46 85; www. parapentegrancanariaclubsiroco.com
You don't need to be super-fit to practise this adrenaline sport, but you do need a head for heights. Beginners can try a tandem jump.

5 Skydiving
Skydive Gran Canaria: 928 15 73 25; www.skydivegrancanaria.es
For an alternative view of the Maspalomas dunes, try jumping out of a plane 3,500 m (11,480 ft) above the resort – strapped to an instructor, of course.

6 Jet Skiing
Atlantic Wave: MAP C6; Pasito Blanco; 622 23 03 10

Jet ski tours along the south and west coasts of the island take in caves and secluded beaches. For more marine activities see pp52–3.

7 Canyoning
Canariaventura: 928 76 61 68; www.canariaventura.com

If you want to get to know parts of the island untouched by most visitors, you could take an excursion that includes hiking through dense vegetation and lowering yourself into rocky clefts. The varied terrain of the island makes it the perfect place for both novices and experienced canyoners alike.

Cycling along a coastal path

8 Cycling
Free Motion: 928 77 74 79; www.free-motion.com

Hardcore cyclists lap up the challenge posed by the island's mountain roads. Join an organized group tour or just hire your own bike (see p109).

9 Horse Riding
El Salobre: 616 41 83 63; www.elsalobrehr.es

Although you can ride all year round, the winter months are more pleasant. You can choose 2- or 3-hour tours, which take you into the mountains.

10 Helicopter Rides
Islas Helicopters: 928 157 965 ◼ www.islas-helicopters.com

You can book a 10- to 60-minute helicopter flight for a unique view of the Gran Canarian landscape.

TOP 10 CANARIAN SPORTS STARS

Tennis player Magüi Serna

1 Juan Carlos Valerón
The talented former *Primera Liga* football midfielder Valerón won more than 40 international caps.

2 Luis Doreste
With two Olympic gold medals, Doreste is among Spain's top sailing stars. He's the younger brother of José Luis (see below).

3 Domingo Manrique
This four-time Olympian sailor won a gold medal at Barcelona in 1992 with his team mate Doreste.

4 Adelina Taylor
Taylor was crowned 2001 Spanish and European surfing champion.

5 Magüi Serna
At her peak in the 1990s, she was ranked in the world's top 20 female tennis players.

6 El Pollito de la Frontera
The "Little Chicken" was one of the big names in *Lucha Canaria* (team wrestling in a sand circle) after his mid-1990s debut.

7 Hermanas Ruano
Twin sisters Iballa and Daida regularly rank first and second in international windsurfing competitions.

8 Björn Dunkerbeck
Although Danish originally, this windsurfing star has long lived on the island. He was world champion from 1988 through to 1999.

9 José Luis Doreste
Doreste sailed in every Olympiad from Montreal (1976) to Atlanta (1996), winning gold at Seoul in 1988.

10 Antonio Alfonso (Tonono)
A UD Las Palmas legend, he played in the national team 22 times.

🔟 Children's Attractions

Visitors enjoying the Pirate's River at Aqualand Maspalomas

1 Water Parks

MAP C5 ■ Aqualand Maspalomas, Ctra Palmitos Park, km 3 ■ 928 14 05 25 ■ Open 10am–5pm daily (Jul–Aug 10am–6pm) ■ Adm ■ www.aqualand.es/maspalomas

There are 33 slides at Aqualand Maspalomas, the largest water park on the island. There is a smaller water park in the southwestern resort of Taurito.

2 Palmitos Park

The Chamoriscan ravine provides a marvellous setting for this tropical paradise, home to primates, reptiles and countless exotic birds. Regular shows feature parrots and enormous birds of prey. Other options include the aquarium, butterfly house and a large walk-through birdcage. The restaurant serves traditional Canarian food alongside more international offerings (see p102).

3 Sioux City Park, San Agustín

Spend a day in the Wild West and experience daring bank hold-ups, stampeding cattle and sudden shoot-outs. Friday night is barbecue night, when parents can enjoy the saloon and dancing girls, while the children are treated to a lasso show (see p101).

4 Museo Elder de la Ciencia y la Tecnología, Las Palmas

When you arrive and see the mottos "Forbidden not to touch" and "Museum is not mausoleum", you know the kids are going to enjoy themselves. Favourites include the flight simulator, TV studio and Imax cinema. There is also a science-themed play area for the smallest visitors, aged 3–6 (see p44 & p73).

5 Yellow Submarine, Puerto de Mogán

MAP B5 ■ 928 56 51 08 ■ Boats leave hourly 10am–5pm daily ■ Adm ■ No disabled access ■ www.atlantidasubmarine.com

Descend 25 m (82 ft) below the surface of the waves on a 45-minute journey that takes in a shipwreck and diverse marine life.

6 Angry Birds Activity Park

MAP B5 ■ Avenida la Cornisa, 2, Puerto Rico ■ 928 15 39 76 ■ Open 10am–8pm Mon–Fri, 11am–9pm Fri–Sat ■ Adm

A theme park based on the popular video game, featuring an adventure playground with trampolines, mini go-karts, rides and arcade games. An ideal spot for younger children.

⑦ Cocodrilo Park, Corralillos

MAP E4 ▪ GC-104, Ctra Los Coralillos, km 5 ▪ 928 78 47 25 ▪ Open 10am–5pm Sun–Fri (parrot show: noon; crocodile feeding: 1pm) ▪ Adm

Europe's largest crocodile sanctuary is also a haven for other mistreated animals. There are over 300 crocodiles, tropical and Canarian fish, other reptiles, tarantulas, a parrot show and a family of tigers.

⑧ Hangar37

MAP E5 ▪ Carretera General del Sur km 45 (behind Gran Karting Club), Tarajalillo ▪ 669 82 92 33 ▪ Open 10am–8pm Sat–Mon, 3–8pm Tue–Fri ▪ Adm

Airsoft combat in a realistic war zone with tanks, jeeps, aircraft and an assortment of tunnels and bunkers.

⑨ Gran Karting Club

MAP E5 ▪ Ctra General del Sur, km 46 ▪ 928 15 71 90 ▪ Open 11am–10pm daily ▪ Adm ▪ www.grankartingclub.es

Family fun with everything from mini cars for toddlers to pint-sized motorbikes and full-size go-karts.

Lights of Holiday World, Maspalomas

⑩ Holiday World, Maspalomas

MAP D6 ▪ Avda Touroperador Tui ▪ 928 73 04 98 ▪ Open 6–11pm Sun–Thu, 6pm–midnight Fri–Sat (summer), 5–11pm Sun–Thu, 5pm–midnight Fri–Sat (winter) ▪ Adm

A funfair with carousels, bumper cars and a roller coaster that lights up the sky in the south of the island.

TOP 10 TIPS FOR FAMILIES

Children playing on the beach

1 Sun
Use high-factor sunblock and keep kids out of the midday sun.

2 Sightseeing
Under-12s often get half-price entry, and children under the age of 5 go free. Ask about family tickets.

3 Beaches
For a safer swim, head for the calm waters off the resorts of Las Canteras and Arguineguín.

4 Noise
Canarians are incredibly tolerant of noise, so don't worry about your kids getting rowdy – except in churches.

5 Car Hire
If you need a child or baby seat, book in advance, as smaller companies may have limited numbers available.

6 Escape the Resorts
As an alternative to resort attractions, consider horse riding in the mountains, or visiting the capital's parks.

7 Boat Trips
The best options are glass-bottomed vessels or those that offer watersports.

8 Accommodation
An extra bed for a child under 12 is usually half price and a cot is usually gratis. Younger children often go free.

9 Restaurants
Canarians love children, although upmarket places may be wary of accepting them, especially in the evening. Children's portions aren't usually available.

10 Quiet Towns
Small town centres such as Teror, Firgas and Agüimes are virtually traffic-free, so you can feel safer about your children wandering around.

🔟 Restaurants

The bright interior of fine-dining restaurant 360° Bohemia

① 360° Bohemia
MAP D6 ■ Avda Estados Unidos 28, Playa del Inglés ■ 928 56 34 00 ■ €€

Gourmet cuisine from Chef Xavier Franquet, with 360° views over the Maspalomas dunes. Allow time for a pre-dinner cocktail on the terrace and opt for the taster menu for the full experience.

② La Palmera Sur
MAP D6 ■ C/Plácido Domingo 12, Maspalomas ■ 659 59 80 03 ■ Closed Sun & Mon ■ €€

This lovely little place, disguised as a café and hidden away in the Bellavista housing estate at the back of the resort, serves deliciously creative cuisine to locals and tourists.

La Palmera Sur, a hidden gem

③ Casa Brito
Traditional decor, great service and a wood-burning grill provide the sights and tastes of rustic Gran Canaria. This popular restaurant in Arucas is something of a local institution (see p85).

④ El Capita
MAP B2 ■ C/Nstra Sñra de las Nieves 3, Puerto de las Nieves ■ 928 55 41 42 ■ €

A great little fish and seafood restaurant. Waiters will recommend best fish of the day, and the paella is definitely worth the half-hour wait.

⑤ El Encuentro
Good-quality food, with views over the church in the plaza in Teror. The menu is largely typical Canarian fare, but be sure to try their excellent salads and leave room for dessert. The place can get very busy at lunchtimes, so book ahead (see p91).

⑥ De Cuchara, Las Palmas
MAP P2 ■ C/Alfredo L Jones 37 ■ 928 26 55 09 ■ Closed Mon ■ €€

A refreshing mix of Canarian classics is served alongside more international dishes at this family-run joint. Desserts include the local *huevos mole*, which is a cold pudding made of egg yolks.

(7) Deliciosa Marta
MAP J5 ▪ C/Pérez Galdós 23, Las Palmas ▪ 928 37 08 82 ▪ Closed Sat & Sun ▪ €€

Located on one of the most attractive streets of the capital, this is the number one restaurant in Las Palmas, and possibly on the whole island. Michelin-standard food, lovely surroundings and absolutely first-class service.

(8) Restaurante Tagoror, Barranco de Guayadeque
MAP E4 ▪ Montaña Las Tierras 21 ▪ 928 17 20 13 ▪ €

Although it is on the tourist trail, Tagoror's food remains true to its origins, and its prices are low. A series of tunnels connects the rooms, all hewn out of the mountainside. Every Canarian favourite graces the menu: try *gofio*, the chorizo, or the goat stew.

Dine in a cave at Restaurante Tagoror

(9) Calma Chicha
MAP D6 ▪ Avda de Tirajana 4, Playa del Inglés ▪ 928 76 07 14 ▪ Closed Sun D ▪ €€

Top-notch Spanish cuisine is served in this cosy restaurant. An intimate interior fills quickly in winter, and there's a nice outdoor terrace for warmer nights. Booking is advised.

(10) Samsara
MAP D6 ▪ Avda del Oasis 30, Maspalomas ▪ 928 14 27 36 ▪ Closed Mon ▪ €

A wonderful Thai-themed fusion restaurant, where the white plates can be personalized to convey messages to loved ones.

TOP 10 CANARIAN DISHES

Mojo, a spicy Canarian sauce

1 Ropa Vieja
Originally a way to use up leftovers, this chickpea (*garbanzo*) stew is now a firm favourite among Canarios.

2 Papas Arrugadas
The ubiquitous side order: these are small potatoes boiled in their skins in very salty water.

3 Mojo
Spicy sauces, heavy on garlic, once used to hide the taste of unappetizing food. The red sauce usually goes with meat and potatoes, while the green version accompanies fish.

4 Gofio
A blend of roasted maize, barley or wheat, served in a variety of ways. This is probably the only food surviving from Guanche times, and something of an acquired taste.

5 Bienmesabe
Often eaten with ice cream, Bienmesabe is an exceptionally sweet sauce, containing almonds, honey and sugar. The name is also given to a cake with the same ingredients.

6 Potaje de Berros
Stew made with watercress, vegetables and sometimes meat. All Canarians have their own recipe.

7 Queso de Flor
Goat's or sheep's cheese mixed with a blue thistle flower; a speciality of Guía.

8 Chorizo de Teror
Locals love sandwiches made with this exceedingly garlicky sausage.

9 Carne de Cabra
The staple meat of the Guanches, goat is still a favourite on Canarian menus.

10 Bizcocho
A lovely light, fluffy sponge cake.

For a key to restaurant price ranges see p79

🔟 Places to Shop

1 Mercadillo de Santa Brígida

MAP E3 ■ Under Municipal Park
■ Open 8am–8pm Sat, 8am–2pm Sun

Stock up your picnic hamper at this farmers' market. Along with locally grown fruit and vegetables, there are first-rate cheeses and fresh bread. Get a handmade wooden toy for the little ones and a well-crafted walking stick to help you hike in the hills.

Stall at Mercadillo de San Fernando

2 Mercadillo de San Fernando

MAP D6 ■ C/San Mateo
■ Open 8am–2pm Wed & Sun

One of the south's "big three" markets along with Puerto de Mogán and Arguineguín; 400 stalls of clothes, souvenirs and local produce vie for attention. Inside the hall you'll find freshly juiced fruits, home-made cakes and speciality foods such as German bratwurst.

3 Mercadillo de Santa Lucía de Tirajana

MAP D4 ■ Plaza Santa Lucía
■ Open 8am–2pm Sun

Head to the centre of Santa Lucía de Tirajana for the freshest local produce at bargain prices. Pick up the town's speciality products, such as its olives and its *mejunje de ventura*, made from a recipe of honey rum with herbs.

4 Mercadillo de Arguineguín

MAP C6 ■ C/Paco González
■ Open 8am–2pm Tue

A popular market selling the usual array of souvenirs, and anything from fake designer labels and leather goods to African drums and bikinis.

5 Mercado de Artesanía y Cultura de Vegueta

MAP M5 ■ Plaza del Pilar
■ Open 10am–3pm Sun

Artisans gather in the streets behind the cathedral to sell ceramics, clothing, food and handicrafts. Stop for refreshments in one of the make-shift bars set up for the occasion and watch the folk-dancing display.

6 Shopping Centres

El Muelle and Las Arenas in Las Palmas are both well equipped with chain stores and places to eat. Other popular centres are Varadero in Meloneras, Las Terrazas in Telde and Tropical in Playa del Inglés.

El Muelle Shopping Centre

Produce at Mercadillo de San Mateo

7 Mercadillo de San Mateo

The island's best farmers' market offers excellent local produce and local handicrafts, such as wicker work and leather goods. Try the marinated olives and *pan de millo* (sweet yellow cornbread; *see p90*).

8 Calle Mayor de Triana, Las Palmas

The Modernist buildings that line the city's most elite shopping street now house chain stores, such as Benetton and Marks & Spencer, but it's still a great place to while away an afternoon. For unique purchases, head to the boutiques in the cobbled side streets, where you'll find one-off clothes shops, original handicrafts and specialist bookshops *(see p77)*.

9 Vecindario
MAP E5

The island's third-largest town is no beauty, but it has two large malls, and a high street stretching 3 km (2 miles). Visit the big chain stores, or the craft shop in Parque de la Era de Verdugo.

10 The Mint Company, Meloneras

MAP D6 ■ Avda Paseo Playa s/n, CC Boulevard El Faro
■ Open 10:15am–10pm daily
■ www.themintcompany.com

Pick up great fashion bargains at this popular store selling top brands at low prices. It also offers a good personal shopping service and Wi-Fi.

TOP 10 SOUVENIRS

1 Cheese
Buy *queso de flor* (flower cheese), a speciality of Santa Maria de Guía.

2 Lacework and Embroidery
Buy embroidered tablecloths, pretty place mats and blouses in Ingenio.

3 Pottery
The only Guanche tradition to have survived is the production of hand-crafted ceramics. Potters still make their wares without a wheel in La Atalaya, Hoya de Pineda and Juncalillo.

4 Mojo
You should take home at least two jars of the spicy sauce: one green and one red *(see p63)*.

5 Timples
This small, five-stringed instrument resembles a ukulele and is the musical emblem of the island. A few artisans still make it by hand.

6 Mejunje de ventura
If dark rum is too hard to swallow, go for a bottle of honey rum instead.

7 Pintaderas
Necklaces of replica Guanche *pintaderas* (ceramic stamps) make beautiful and original gifts.

8 Agaete Coffee
Strong coffee, grown in the Agaete Valley, is on sale across the island.

9 Aloe Vera
The healing plant grows in abundance on the island, so Gran Canaria is a great place to stock up on cosmetics made from its extracts.

10 Traditional Costume
You'll probably never wear it, but the traditional island dress is very interesting visually and also makes a rather good wall hanging.

Pottery on sale in Fataga

📟 Gran Canaria for Free

1 Ruta Playa Viva
MAP H2

Every Saturday evening, at outdoor venues along the promenade of Las Canteras beach, half a dozen or more bands perform live sets. From cover versions of classic rock to improvised jazz, this free street festival is a great way for everyone to enjoy the sunset over the beach.

2 Museums and Galleries

Some are free to enter all the time, but most have days when they drop the charge. This varies depending on individual museums and galleries, but many, including all the major Las Palmas museums and Cueva Pintada, are free on the first weekend of each month. Check individual websites for further admission details.

3 Traditional Music and Dance
MAP J4 ■ C/Francisco González Días, Las Palmas ■ 928 24 29 85

Canarian folklore is an important part of Gran Canaria's culture, and you can see local bands and dance groups dressed in traditional costume performing for free at the Pueblo Canario in Las Palmas each Sunday, and in other fiestas across the island (see pp68–9).

Dancers dressed in traditional costumes

4 Historic Town Tours
www.grancanaria.com

The Gran Canaria Tourist Board website offers free podcast tours in English for a range of historic towns, such as Tejeda, Teror, Arucas and Las Palmas, as well as villages including Santa Lucía de Tirajana. They cover history, culture and all the most important sights. Download iPhone/iPad or Android apps from their website.

Parque Doramas in Las Palmas

5 Parks and Gardens
Parque Doramas: MAP J4
■ Parque Botanico de Maspalomas: MAP D6

From leafy plazas and beautiful gardens to botanical masterpieces, Gran Canaria's subtropical splendour often comes without a price tag. The best are Jardín Botanico Viera y Clavijo (see pp18–19), Parque Doramas and Parque Botanico de Maspalomas.

6 Hiking

An intricate network of *caminos reales* (royal pathways), linking the various municipalities, makes Gran Canaria perfect for trekking. Try the three-day Camino de Santiago hike from Playa del Inglés to Gáldar. For a shorter, family-friendly walk, choose the path from La Goleta car park to Roque Nublo.

Stargazing

Canarian skies are among the clearest in the world, and you don't have to go on a guided tour to appreciate them. Just choose a moonless night and head to the upper reaches of the interior for a vantage point above the clouds and away from the lights of the south coast.

8 **Camping**
www.gobcan.es/cmayot/
There are over a dozen free camp sites across the island, and some are in beauty spots such as Tamadaba and the Cuevas de las Niñas lake. Most have only a few amenities. You must have prior written permission, which you should apply for online and must collect in person from Las Palmas.

Camping with a view in Tamadaba

9 **Beaches**
You don't have to pay out for a sun lounger; find a spot away from the regimented rows and just throw a towel onto the sand. As all beaches in Spain are public by law, you can find your own piece of paradise.

10 **Fiestas**
All the local fiestas and some of the island's biggest events, such as Carnival, are open to one and all. Most towns and villages stage an annual *romería* (a celebratory pilgrimage), usually in the summer months, all of them offering a free day of music, dancing and fun.

TOP 10 MONEY-SAVING TIPS

Set lunch menus are great value

1 Follow Vegueta's "Ruta de Tapas" every Thursday; you pay €2 for a tapa and drink at each bar participating in the scheme.

2 Save money and avoid the crowds by booking off-peak. The most expensive periods are between November and Easter, and during the summer school holidays.

3 Most of the island's restaurants offer Menu del Día lunchtime deals for between €6 and €9.

4 Buy a *bono de guagua* (Las Palmas) or *tarjeta insular* for generously discounted bus fares.

5 Consider investing in an LPA card, which allows you free entry to 20 participating museums. For more information, visit www.lpacard.com/en/laspalmascard

6 Head to the *rebajas* (sales) for fashion bargains, from January to March and July to August.

7 Shop at farmers' markets and supermarkets, such as Mercadona and Hiperdino, for the best savings on fresh produce and other groceries.

8 Save money and the planet by buying 5L or 8L water carriers and refilling small bottles.

9 Canarios like to serve generous food portions at reasonable prices; you'll find these at traditional restaurants outside big resort centres.

10 Wines, handicrafts and souvenirs are all much cheaper on the island than at the airport, so stock up before you begin your journey home.

TOP 10 Traditional Fiestas

Cabalgata de los Reyes Magos

1 Cabalgata de los Reyes Magos (Procession of the Three Kings)
5 Jan, Las Palmas

Melchior, Balthazar and Caspar ride through the capital's streets on camels, throwing sweets to children, who later receive presents from the kings. Shops open until 2am for late-night gift-buying, and there are parties in the streets and makeshift bars in Triana.

2 Carnaval
Feb–Mar, island-wide

Don your best costume and get ready for 2 months of *murgas* (satirical singing), *comparsas* (dancing competitions) and the all-important crowning of the drag queen. The party culminates in the burial of the sardine, a bizarre spectacle with mock mourners weeping because their fun has ended for another year.

Murgas **performance at Carnaval**

3 Semana Santa (Holy Week)
Mar–Apr, island-wide

This is a sombre affair, featuring solemn processions silencing towns across the island. On Good Friday, Las Palmas women don traditional dress and carry a sculpture of Christ along red carpets in Vegueta. There are similar processions island-wide on Easter Sunday, though none is quite as emotionally charged as the equivalent in mainland Spain.

4 Día de Canarias (Canary Islands Day)
30 May, island-wide

Although relatively new, this commemoration of Canarian autonomy celebrates all that is time-honoured in the islands. Traditional costume is obligatory, and merrymakers play the *timple* (a small guitar) and dance as their ancestors did. Local food and drink are dished out freely, so this is a great time for a visit.

5 Fiesta de San Juan
23–24 Jun, Las Palmas and other places

Revellers leap over bonfires and throw oranges into the ocean, while fireworks light up the sky. Celebrated with gusto on Playa de Las Canteras, as well as in Arucas and Telde, the festival coincides with the founding of Las Palmas, so the celebrations in the capital are particularly impressive.

⑥ Corpus Christi
Jun, Las Palmas and other towns across the island

The tradition of flower-petal carpets has been lost in many parts of Spain, but it is still firmly a part of Canarian culture. Don't miss the mammoth carpet laid out in front of Las Palmas cathedral – it's always a wonderful work of art.

⑦ Bajada de la Rama (Taking Down of the Branches)
4–5 Aug, Agaete and Puerto de las Nieves

This is a colourful pre-Hispanic rain-making ritual, in which locals parade to the ocean and beat the water with pine branches.

⑧ Fiesta de Nuestra Señora del Pino (Festival of Our Lady of the Pine)
8 Sep, Teror

The pretty town of Teror is the setting for this party honouring the Canary Islands' patron saint *(see pp26–7)*.

Locals enjoying the Fiesta del Charco

⑨ Fiesta del Charco
11 Sep, Puerto de la Aldea

This lively Guanche festival sees participants wade through the murky waters of the *charco* (a large pond) to catch fish with their bare hands. It is messy but strangely good fun.

⑩ Romerías
Year-round, island-wide

Each town or village hosts its own *romería* (pilgrimage), which is really a street party featuring traditional dancing and Canarian food.

TOP 10 CONTEMPORARY FESTIVALS

Performance at Jazz & Más

1 Opera Festival, Las Palmas
Feb–Jun
The Alfredo Kraus Auditorium hosts an impressive programme of operas.

2 Film Festival, Las Palmas
Mar
Week-long festival of independent and mainstream films across the capital.

3 Masdanza, Maspalomas
Oct
Contemporary dance festival with shows and workshops.

4 Fiesta del Queso, Guía
April/May
Sample Canarian culture as well as local cheese at this popular festival.

5 Gay Pride, Maspalomas
May
Exhibitions, fundraisers and a big street parade promote equal rights.

6 Feria del Caballo, Valsequillo
May
This horse festival is the island's most important agricultural celebration.

7 International Folklore Festival, Ingenio
July
Global music and dance celebrating Ingenio's multicultural citizens.

8 Jazz & Más, Las Palmas
July
The capital becomes a (mostly open-air) stage for international jazz.

9 Traída del Agua, Lomo Magullo
First half of Aug
This huge annual water-fight has a history that goes back centuries.

10 Traída del Barro
July
Partygoers make hay in clay, at La Atalaya, the island's pottery capital.

Gran Canaria
Area by Area

The imposing façade of Casa de Colón

🔟 Las Palmas

Las Palmas can date its beginnings from the day Juan Rejón landed at La Isleta and earmarked the area for his settlement *(see p38)*. The arrival of Christopher Columbus, the increase in maritime traffic, and, finally, the construction of the port, guaranteed success as a trading hub. Today Las Palmas is the Canary Islands' biggest city, with a vibrant ethnic mix, reflecting its position as a crossroads between Africa, Europe and Latin America. A paradise for shopaholics, Las Palmas also has leafy suburbs and quiet cobbled streets, all crowned by Playa de Las Canteras, one of the world's top city beaches.

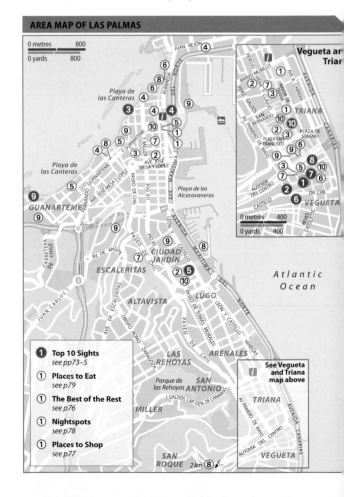

AREA MAP OF LAS PALMAS

1 Top 10 Sights
see pp73–5

① Places to Eat
see p79

① The Best of the Rest
see p76

① Nightspots
see p78

① Places to Shop
see p77

1 Catedral de Santa Ana

Las Palmas' enormous Santa Ana cathedral and adjoining sacred art museum contain some important paintings and sculptures dating back to the 16th century, including two woodcarvings by renowned 18th- to 19th-century local sculptor José Luján Pérez *(see pp14–15)*.

2 Casas Consistoriales

MAP M5 ■ Plaza de Santa Ana ■ Open 9am–6pm Mon–Fri, 10am–2pm Sat & Sun

Taking centre stage in Plaza de Santa Ana and guarded by its faithful bronze hounds is the magnificent 19th-century Neo-Classical Casas Consistoriales. Built on the site of the original 16th-century Town Hall, which burned down in 1842, the edifice houses some 90 works of art by Canarian artists, including César Manrique. Perhaps the highlight is one of Álvarez Sala's famous *Emigrantes* paintings, which hangs above the main staircase.

3 Playa de Las Canteras

MAP N2

Few cities can boast a beach as good as Playa de Las Canteras: 3 km (2 miles) of fine sand, sandwiched between a wide promenade and the chilly Atlantic Ocean. Surfers tend to congregate at the western end, an area known as La Cicer. The sand here is black, but as you move

eastwards it becomes ever more golden, and the sea, protected by the broad reef, takes on the appearance of a lake. Locals sometimes head for *el ascensor* ("the lift"), a part of the reef where the swell catapults swimmers back up onto the rocks – the really sure way to spot it is to look for the throng of whooping youngsters in front of Playa Chica.

Exhibits at Museo Elder de la Ciencia

4 Museo Elder de la Ciencia y la Tecnología

MAP P2 ■ Parque Santa Catalina ■ 828 01 18 28 ■ Open 10am–8pm Tue–Sun ■ Adm ■ www.museoelder.org

While kids enjoy the many interactive exhibits, parents might prefer to find out how beer is made, what they would weigh on Mars, or if their hearing and heartbeat are normal. This is a great place to spend a few hours, especially if you're caught in the rain in Las Palmas.

Sun-worshippers gather on Playa de Las Canteras

⑤ Museo Néstor

MAP J4 ▪ Pueblo Canario ▪ 928 24 51 35 ▪ Open 10am–7pm Tue–Sat, 10:30am–2:30pm Sun and public hols ▪ Adm

Las Palmas-born artist Néstor Martín Fernández de la Torre is (1887–1938) best known as a Modernist painter, but you can also see evidence of Pre-Raphaelitism and Symbolism in his colourful works. Construction of the Neo-Canarian building housing the gallery was a joint project by the artist and his architect brother Miguel. As well as Néstor's famous "poems", huge paintings comprising eight panels each, there are some vivid sketches based on theatre productions. Towards the end of his life, Néstor favoured pictures depicting hidden corners of his beloved Gran Canaria, in a style he called "Typism" (see p45).

⑥ Museo Canario

This museum boasts the largest collection of Guanche artifacts to be found anywhere and provides a fascinating insight into their culture. This is a good preparation for those who may be visiting Guanche sites around the island (see pp16–17).

⑦ Casa de Colón

The main focus of this first-rate museum is Christopher Columbus's travels across the Atlantic and their effect on the Canary Islands. Pre-Columbian cultures and historic Las Palmas are rewarding subsidiary themes. It's all displayed in a beautiful restored Canarian house (see pp12–13).

⑧ Vegueta Architecture

MAP M5

A stroll around the capital's oldest district is a must for its quiet cobbled streets and varied architecture. Unfortunately, pirate attacks in the 16th century destroyed much of the original hamlet set up after the Conquest, but there is still plenty to see. Balconies prevail, be they the wooden-box-like designs favoured in Canarian architecture or the more ornate wrought-iron versions typical of Modernist buildings.

Casa de Colón's elaborate entrance

9 Auditorio Alfredo Kraus

MAP G3 ▪ Avda Príncipe de Asturias s/n ▪ 928 49 17 70 ▪ Guided tours are available for groups ▪ Adm ▪ www.auditorioteatro laspalmasgc.es

One of the city's landmark buildings, this fine modern auditorium, perched on the jetty at the western end of Playa de Las Canteras, hosts cultural events, including the opera season, the film festival and jazz concerts. If the productions here are not to your taste, you can always admire the stunning ocean view.

The modern Auditorio Alfredo Kraus

10 Triana

Not long after the Conquest, the original Vegueta settlement became too small for the island's increasing population and spread across the Guiniguada ravine. By the 19th century, the neighbouring district of Triana was a bustling area, featuring some fine architecture and a large theatre. It was formerly the elite that shopped on the city's premiere street, Calle Mayor de Triana, but these days, affordable chain stores complement the exclusive boutiques. Do venture away from the main street, for it is in the side streets that you will find Triana's real treasures – such as one-off handicraft shops and snug *tapas* bars. There's more to Triana than shopping, though: admire the exquisite architecture of the Gabinete Literario, the Teatro Pérez Galdós *(see pp40–41)*, and also the Ermita de San Telmo *(see p47)*.

LAS PALMAS PAST AND PRESENT

▶ MORNING

Any walk around the capital should begin where *it* did, in the Vegueta *barrio*. Start at the **Palacio de Justicia**, on Avda Marítima, and head into the old town via a narrow alley to the right of the courts; just a 17th-century tower remains of the original building. Pass the impressive stone archway of the Jesuit Iglesia de San Francisco de Borja as you make your way to the must-see **Museo Canario**.

From the museum, head to the **Plaza and Ermita de Espíritu Santo**, then double back again to the **Cathedral de Santa Ana** *(see p73)* and the **Casas Consistoriales** in Plaza de Santa Ana. Head across the main road to the **Triana** district, en route admiring the Italianate Neo-Classical **Teatro Pérez Galdós** *(see p40)*, and have lunch at **Allende Triana** *(see p79)*.

AFTERNOON

After lunch, make for C/Mayor de Triana to shop for souvenirs and clothes. Head north to **Parque San Telmo**, where there's a bus station. Here you can jump on a *guagua* to cross the city, unless you relish the idea of a 45-minute stroll along the promenade. Alight at **Parque de Santa Catalina**, heading first to the **Centro de Arte La Regenta** *(see p76)*, a contemporary art museum, and then to the **Museo Elder de la Ciencia y la Tecnología**, before ending the day at **Playa de Las Canteras**. Get an artisan ice cream from **Peña la Vieja** on the Paseo de Las Canteras.

See map on p72 ←

The Best of the Rest

1 Parque and Ermita de San Telmo
MAP L4

A leafy respite in Triana's shopping centre. The kiosk is Art Nouveau and the altar in the 18th-century Ermita de San Telmo is considered one of the prettiest on the island.

Fountains at Parque Doramas

2 Parque Doramas
MAP J4 ▪ C/Emilio Ley

The city's prettiest park is named after the Guanche leader who refused to bow to the Spanish. It's well equipped for children and has a small open-air café.

3 Casa Museo Pérez Galdós
MAP L5 ▪ C/Cano 2 ▪ 928 36 69 76 ▪ Open 10am–2pm, 4–8pm Tue–Fri, 10am–2pm Sat–Sun (guided tours only, every hour) ▪ www.casamuseoperezgaldos.com

Novelist Benito Pérez Galdós – "the Spanish Charles Dickens" – is the island's most famous former inhabitant. His charming childhood home in Triana is now a museum.

4 Castillo de la Luz
MAP Q1 ▪ C/Juan Rejón s/n

The 16th-century fort overlooks a popular children's playground. Set in a small park equipped with a cheap café serving tasty food, it's also a fine place to while away an afternoon.

5 Centro de Arte La Regenta
MAP P3 ▪ C/León y Castillo 427 ▪ 928 11 74 68 ▪ Open Tue–Fri 11am–2pm, 5–8pm, Sat 11am–2pm ▪ Closed Sun & Mon

Housed in a former tobacco ware-house, La Regenta is a treasure trove of contemporary art, and mounts numerous exhibitions every year.

6 CAAM
MAP M5 ▪ C/Los Balcones 11 ▪ 928 31 18 00 ▪ Open 10am–9pm Tue–Sat, 10am–2pm Sun ▪ www.caam.net

Vegueta's most modern space, the Neo-Classical Centro Atlántico de Arte Moderno hosts contemporary sculptures, paintings and video art.

7 Vistas from Escaleritas
MAP H4

You'll get the best view of the city's port, beaches, skyscrapers and palm trees from the Escaleritas *barrio*.

8 Muelle Deportivo
MAP J3

The sporting marina attracts sailors from across the globe. Many come to rest before heading to southern Africa or across the Atlantic.

9 Ciudad Jardín
MAP H3

As you enter "Garden City", the unsightly skyscrapers of Las Palmas' commercial districts give way to grand mansions, mostly built by British settlers in the 19th and early 20th centuries and now home to the city's wealthiest families.

10 Pueblo Canario
MAP J4 ▪ C/Francisco González Díaz ▪ Open 10am–midnight Tue–Sat, 10:30am–5pm Sun

Built in the mid-20th century, this miniature Canarian village is a good place to sample local cuisine, buy handicrafts or admire the work of Néstor de la Torre *(see p45)*.

Places to Shop

① Calle Mayor de Triana
MAP L4

Although Avda de Mesa y López is vying for the position of top shopping street, Triana still has the charm.

② El Corte Inglés
MAP P3

If you can't find what you're looking for in this mammoth department store, it may well not exist. There are two branches on Avda de José Mesa y López and a third in the 7 Palmas shopping centre.

③ FEDAC
MAP L4 ■ C/Domingo J Navarro 7

The best artisans from across the island sell their wares in this non-profit outlet in Triana.

④ Artesanía Santa Catalina
MAP P3 ■ C/Ripoche 4

This is a good place to hunt for typical Canarian souvenirs. The speciality is pottery, but you will also find foodstuffs, aloe vera products and embroidered goods.

⑤ Tienda Artesania Canaria Las Palmitas
MAP M5 ■ C/Herrería 7, Vegueta

The perfect place to pick up an interesting souvenir or gift, while at the same time supporting local artisans. The shop is crammed with handicrafts, from wooden jewellery to earthenware jugs.

⑥ Las Canteras Lifestyle
MAP H1 ■ Paseo de Las Canteras 20

The perfect stop to prepare for a day spent at the beach. This handily-placed store stocks stylish bags, hats, and towels.

⑦ El Puente
MAP L5 ■ C/Obispo Codina 6

This charming shop stocks typical Canarian crafts such as tablecloths, pottery and traditional costumes.

⑧ La Casa de Los Quesos
MAP H1 ■ C/Sagasta 32

A gourmet's dream shop, this is *the* place to shop for the island's best artisan cheeses, as well as its wines, *mojos*, honey, coffee and olive oil.

⑨ Malls
La Ballena: MAP G6 C/General del Norte 112 ■ 7 Palmas: MAP E2 Avda Pintor Felo Monzón ■ Monopol: MAP L5 Plaza de Hurtado Mendoza 1 ■ El Muelle: MAP P2 Muelle de Santa Catalina ■ Las Arenas: MAP G3 C/Pavía 12 ■ La Minilla: MAP H3 C/Pintor Juan Guillermo 6–8 ■ Las Ramblas: MAP G4 Avda Juan Carlos I 29 ■ Tamarana: MAP E2 Avda César Manrique s/n ■ El Mirador: MAP F2 Autovía GC-1, Km 5

Las Palmas has no fewer than nine shopping malls.

Shopping mall El Muelle

⑩ La Librería
MAP L4 ■ C/Cano 24

Every aspect of Canarian culture, from hiking and history to festivals and flora, is represented in the *cabildo*'s bookshop in Triana. Although most titles are in Spanish, a few have been translated into other European languages.

See map on p72 ←

Nightspots

Visitors savour the view from La Azotea de Benito's rooftop terrace

1 Fortuni
MAP H2 ■ C/Martínez de Escobar 1

With its retro design but chic and contemporary styling, this venue in the heart of the capital has certainly made a name for itself. Expect live singers, top DJs and a lively party atmosphere.

2 Charleston Café
MAP L4 ■ C/Buenos Aires 14

Acoustic concerts and absinthe give this late-night café a bohemian air. It attracts a friendly, relaxed crowd.

3 Te Lo Dije Perez
MAP L5 ■ C/Obispo Codina 6

In trendy Vegueta, this traditional bar is the favourite haunt of musicians headlining at Teatro Pérez Galdós across the street and is a good place to start the night with a beer.

4 Ruta Playa Viva
MAP H1–H2

Head to Las Canteras beach every Saturday night for a string of free concerts, from rock to jazz, at venues dotted along the promenade. It's a relaxed festival atmosphere enjoyed by families and clubbers alike.

5 NYC Taxi Bar
MAP G3 ■ C/Numancia 25

A small place with very loud music, this lively rock bar is decorated and run like a New York City taxi bar. Order cold beers by the bucket and party like a New Yorker.

6 La Azotea de Benito
MAP L5 ■ CC Monopol, Plaza Hurtado de Mendoza

Catch the last rays of sun at this chic bar on the roof of Centro Commercial (CC) Monopol. Enjoy chill-out sounds in the background and one of the Cocoa Negroni cocktails in hand.

7 Pool Fiction
MAP P3 ■ C/Secretario Artiles 22

Equipped with eight pool tables, a dartboard and a plasma TV, this sophisticated joint behind Parque Santa Catalina is the perfect place for a sporting night out.

8 Las Brujas
MAP E2 ■ Barranco Seco

Outside the city on the way to Tafira, a huge rural house has been converted into an amazing nightspot. You can have a bite to eat in one of the dining rooms dotted about the house, or party in the DJ tent. In summer, revellers spill out into the garden.

9 Paper Club
MAP L5 ■ C/Remedios 10–12

One of Las Palmas' best concert venues, Paper Club attracts a young crowd of devoted revellers.

10 Malecón de la Habana
MAP P3 ■ C/José Franchy Roca

This is one of the best places in the city to hear Latin music, salsa dance and watch live Cuban bands. The place hots up at around 3am.

Places to Eat

PRICE CATEGORIES
For a three-course meal for one with half a bottle of wine (or equivalent meal), taxes and extra charges.

€ under €30   €€ €30–€50   €€€ over €50

1 Rías Bajas
MAP P3 ▪ C/Simón Bolívar 3 ▪ 928 27 13 16 ▪ €€€

The capital's premier restaurant specializes in seafood. If you're daunted by the choice, try the paella or the *arroz caldoso*, a kind of rice stew with lots of seafood.

2 Qué Leche
MAP K5 ▪ C/Torres 22 ▪ 607 91 78 13 ▪ Closed Sun & Mon ▪ €€

A tiny, cosy restaurant with a South American flavour, perfect for sharing inventive tapas, such as squid with pistachio and ginger.

3 Tehran
MAP N3
▪ C/Bernardo de la Torre 1 ▪ 928 22 28 17 ▪ €€

Tehran offers an authentic Iranian experience in terms of cuisine, costumes, Persian decor and even cultural entertainment.

4 Bom Gosto
MAP H2
▪ C/Secretario Padilla 28 ▪ 618 30 85 73 ▪ Closed Mon ▪ €€

For a taste of Portugal close to Playa de Las Canteras, Bom Gasto's menu features the kind of dishes you'd expect to find in a restaurant in Porto, including the meaty, cheesy feast that is a *francesinha*.

5 La Lonja
MAP H2 ▪ C/Galileo 8 ▪ 828 01 44 55 ▪ Closed Tue ▪ €€

A small, friendly, unassuming Canarian *tasca* (or bar) near the

Sushi and sashimi at Fuji

beach. It specializes in fresh fish and seafood, and is a good place to try *arroz caldoso*.

6 Kitchen Lovers
MAP H1 ▪ Paseo de las Canteras 16 ▪ 928 98 76 10 ▪ Closed Mon ▪ €€€

One of the main attractions of this modern Italian restaurant is the views over Las Canteras beach. However, creatively prepared dishes do their best to distract from the golden sands outside the windows.

7 Allende Triana
MAP L4 ▪ C/Domingo J Navarro 16 ▪ 928 38 09 48 ▪ €

The philosophy here is use the best ingredients to create quality dishes from around the world and serve them in comfortably chic surroundings.

8 Fuji
MAP N3 ▪ C/Fernando Guanarteme 56 ▪ 928 26 13 93 ▪ Closed Mon ▪ €€€

Gran Canaria and Spain's first Japanese restaurant, Fuji offers authentic dishes and friendly service. Reserve at the weekend to indulge in delicious sushi and sashimi.

9 Novilla Précoz
MAP H2 ▪ C/de Portugal 9 ▪ 928 22 16 59 ▪ €€€

This Uruguayan restaurant has been serving perfectly cooked steaks to local writers, singers and poets for decades, many of whom have scribbled their names on its walls.

10 Casa Montesdeoca
MAP M5 ▪ C/Montesdeoca 10 ▪ 928 33 34 66 ▪ Closed Sun & Aug ▪ €€€

Succulent steaks and fresh fish are followed by some unique homemade desserts at this atmospheric, traditional Vegueta restaurant.

See map on p72

TOP 10 Northern Gran Canaria

The north is as far removed from the stereotype of the Canary Islands as is possible. The humid climate here blesses the ravines with a layer of lush green vegetation, while rough seas crash against the stony beaches. It's not dream territory for sunbathers or swimmers, but hikers and surfers are certainly well catered for. The cuisine consists of warming meat dishes in the highlands and seafood platters on the coast. The region is also rich in aboriginal remains, since Gáldar was the island's capital before the Europeans invaded.

Statue of La Virgin Carmen in Santa María de Guía

1 Casa-Museo Antonio Padrón, Gáldar

MAP C1 ■ C/Capitán Quesada 3 ■ 928 55 18 58 ■ Open 8am–3pm Mon–Fri ■ www.antoniopadron.com

Born in Gáldar in 1920, Antonio Padrón was a painter, sculptor, ceramicist and composer. Largely known as an Expressionist painter, his work also demonstrates Fauvist tendencies. He portrayed everyday Canarian life, focusing on local myths and customs. Padrón's most familiar works are considered a local treasure.

AREA MAP OF NORTHERN GRAN CANARIA

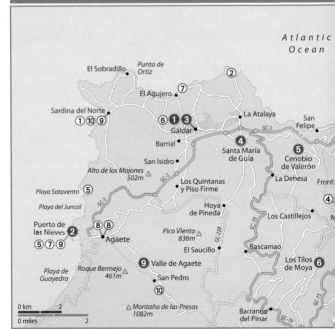

Fishing boats in the harbour at Puerto de las Nieves

2 Puerto de las Nieves

This popular fishing village is full of character. Settle into the slow pace of life here, and enjoy a divine seafood grill overlooking the port *(see pp34–5)*.

1 **Top 10 Sights**
see pp80–83

1 **Places to Eat**
see p85

1 **The Best of the Rest**
see p84

3 Cueva Pintada, Gáldar

MAP C1 ▪ C/Audencia 2, Gáldar ▪ 928 89 54 89 (book in advance) ▪ www.cuevapintada.org

When a farmer from Gáldar discovered a Guanche cave under his land in the 19th century, he could not have realized the magnitude of his find. Archeologists moved in to study the simple paintings adorning its walls – small triangles and squares etched in red and brown. These were soon regarded as the most important set of Guanche engravings in existence, but humidity and human contact began to destroy them. The site was closed in 1982 for a massive restoration project and finally reopened in 2006.

4 Old Quarter, Santa María de Guía

MAP C1

At first glance, Guía has little to offer other than a hotchpotch of modern buildings. Yet, hidden away in its centre, stands a grand Neo-Classical church and one of the island's most charming town centres. The church, begun in 1607, has a clock donated by celebrated sculptor José Luján Pérez, Guía's most famous son. His home, marked by a small plaque, is in a pretty road behind the church. These sleepy, colourful streets ooze character, and the inhabitants are perhaps the friendliest on the island.

WATER CHANNELS

Rainfall is far higher in the north than in the south of the island, but, as the porous ground soaks it up, farmers have had to build irrigation channels, wells, springs and water mills. This impressive hydro-network supports the cultivation of crops in the region, particularly the banana plantations around Arucas. The area's hydraulic heritage can be seen on a hike around Valleseco.

Guanche site Cenobio de Valerón

5 Cenobio de Valerón
MAP D1 ■ GC-291 km 21
■ Open Oct–Mar: 10am–5pm Tue–Sun; Apr–Sep: 10am–6pm Tue–Sun
■ Adm (free for children under 10)
■ www.cenobiodevaleron.com

It's not uncommon to see grain stores on Guanche sites, but none comes close to the Cenobio de Valerón. Located in a cave, this early version of a pantry consists of over 300 hollows, whittled out of the rock face. Although access to it is easy today, the Cenobio was built on an inaccessible crag, to keep food supplies out of the way of thieves. The early theory that the site was a convent, where young girls lived a life of celibacy away from society, has long since been disproved.

6 Los Tilos de Moya
MAP D2 ■ Access via GC-70 and GC-703

Gran Canaria's only natural laurel forest may not be as impressive as those found on other Macronesian islands, but the shady trees are an ideal spot for a hike or picnic. The Canaries' biggest expanse of laurel forest is in La Gomera's national park. Los Tilos de Moya represents about 1 per cent of the once-magnificent Doramas forest. Home to many endangered bird and plant species, it has only a sprinkling of human inhabitants.

7 Parroquia de San Juan Bautista, Arucas
MAP D2 ■ Párroco Cardenes 2
■ 928 60 56 22 ■ Open 9:30am–12:30pm, 4:30–7pm Mon–Sat, 8:30am–1pm, 4:30–7:30pm Sun

Built on the site of an old hermitage, this mammoth Neo-Gothic structure, begun in 1909, took over 60 years to build, and is perhaps the most remarkable church in Gran Canaria. The exquisite stained-glass windows were produced in the 1920s by French designers Frères Mauméjean, and are considered the some of the very best on the island.

8 Parroquia de Nuestra Señora de la Candelaria, Moya
MAP D2 ■ Padre Juanito 9 ■ 928 62 00 07 ■ Open 6–8pm Mon–Sat, 11am–noon, 6–8pm Sun

Clinging precariously to the side of the Moya ravine, this church must have been built by some very brave workmen. Completed in 1957, it is a pleasing blend of towers and roofs of varying heights. The best views are from the GC-700 road from Guía.

Parroquia de Nuestra Señora de la Candelaria

9 Valle de Agaete
MAP C2 ▪ GC-231 from Agaete town centre

So far, even the finest engineers have failed to link the Agaete Valley with the centre of the island, as the steep Tamadaba precipice forbids any possibility of construction. After snaking along the valley, the road fizzles out just after Los Berrazales. Fruit orchards and coffee plantations fill the valley floor, while the Tamadaba pine forest provides a formidable backdrop. There is a magnificent hike on a well-marked path all the way to Artenara, but the walk is more manageable if you start at the other end.

Panorama of the Valle de Agaete

10 Rum Factory, Arehucas
MAP D2 ▪ Era de San Pedro 2 ▪ 928 62 49 00 ▪ Open Mon–Fri 9am–2pm ▪ Closed Sat & Sun

The oldest rum factory in the Canary Islands, operating since 1884, this is the official supplier of the Spanish Royal House. The rum at Arehucas is still distilled the traditional Cuban way, from pressed sugar cane. The factory at Arehucas is more about storage and bottling, with an impressive collection of 6,000 oak barrels, many of them carrying signatures of visiting celebrities. A brief tour of the factory concludes with a tasting session and a chance to buy at discount.

A CULINARY TREK IN NORTHERN GRAN CANARIA

▶ MORNING

If the best way to get to know a place is through its cuisine, then the north is where you'll discover Gran Canaria. Start the day in **Arucas**, allowing half an hour to visit the Parroquia de San Juan Bautista, before taking a guided tour and buying a bottle at the Arehucas rum factory. You'll pass a few remote villages along the GC-300 before reaching **Firgas** (see p84). The unusual town centre has a functioning *gofio* mill, so sampling the most Canarian of all foods (see p63) is a must. Head through the Barranco de Azuaje to **Moya**, where all cafés serve local *suspiros* (meringues) and *bizcochos* (crispy sponge cakes).

AFTERNOON

The road to Guía skirts the laurel forest of **Los Tilos de Moya**. Detour to **Santa María de Guía**; explore the pretty old town and buy the local cheese. Casa Arturo, on C/Lomo Guillén, is the best place to buy *queso de flor* (see p63), generally considered the island's tastiest cheese. Continue on to **Gáldar**, taking in the **Casa-Museo Antonio Padrón** (see p80) and stopping to visit the **Cueva Pintada** (see p81) before joining the GC-202 to **Agaete**. In the village, follow the signs to visit the burial site **Maipés de Arriba** (see p43) and then continue through the **Valle de Agaete** to visit **Bodega Los Berrazales** (see p84), where they produce coffee in the most northerly plantation in the world. Sample their wine and coffee before backtracking to end the day with a swim at **Puerto de Las Nieves** (see pp34–5).

See map on pp80–81 ←

The Best of the Rest

1 Jardín de la Marquesa, Arucas

MAP D2 ■ GC-330, Las Hoyas 2 ■ 928 60 44 86 ■ Open 9am–1pm, 2–6pm Mon–Sat ■ Adm

These impressive botanical gardens, bordering an ornate 19th-century mansion, are home to well over 2,500 species of flora, both native and tropical, and some strutting peacocks.

Plants in the Jardín de la Marquesa

2 Natural Pools

MAP C1 & D1

As the north coast is dangerous for swimmers, town councils have created rock pools that are constantly replenished by the sea. The best are in Bañaderos, San Felipe and Roque Prieto.

3 Firgas Town Centre

MAP D2

Famous for its mineral water, Firgas is also known for its mill. Watch a demonstration and buy a bag of freshly ground *gofio (see p63)*.

4 Casa-Museo Tomás Morales, Moya

MAP D2 ■ Plaza de Tomás Morales ■ 928 62 02 17 ■ Open 10am–8pm Mon–Sun

This museum honours Moya poet Tomás Morales, though for non-Spanish-speakers the interest lies more in seeing inside an upmarket 19th-century home.

5 Hidden Coves

MAP B2, C1 & D1

The north coast is not noted for its beaches, but it has some quiet coves, if you know where to look. The prettiest are on the Gáldar coast, but Playa Sotavento north of Puerto de las Nieves also deserves a visit.

6 Gáldar Architecture

MAP C1

The Iglesia de Santiago de los Caballeros *(see p47)* dominates the pretty plaza, but there are other buildings of interest, such as the eclectic Teatro Municipal, the 19th-century casino, and the town hall, which has a patio that is home to the island's oldest dragon tree.

7 Túmulo de La Guancha

MAP C1 ■ Gáldar to El Agujero road ■ 928 21 94 21 ext 4441 ■ No fixed opening hours; book in advance

This huge, circular construction is Gran Canaria's largest burial site, with 42 tombs radiating from one central grave.

8 Huerto de las Flores, Agaete

MAP C2 ■ C/Huertas ■ Open 9am–2pm Mon–Fri

More than 100 species of tropical plant thrive in this small garden.

9 Sardina del Norte

MAP C1

The fine sandy beach here brings bathers from miles around on sunny weekends, so visit this fishing village midweek if you want to find space to put your towel down.

10 Bodega Los Berrazales, Valle de Agaete

MAP C2 ■ 628 95 25 88 ■ Visit by appointment only

This San Pedro estate of unique beauty is well worth the detour, especially to sample its delicious fare of wine, coffee and the tropical fruits of Agaete Valley.

Places to Eat

PRICE CATEGORIES

For a three-course meal for one with half a bottle of wine (or equivalent meal), taxes and extra charges.

€ under €30   €€ €30–€50   €€€ over €50

1 Marisquería Fragata, Sardina del Norte

MAP C1 ■ Avda Antonio Rosas ■ 928 88 32 96 ■ Closed Sun D, Wed ■ €

This friendly place offers old favourites such as squid and octopus alongside more original choices including gooseneck barnacles.

2 Casa Brito, Visvique

Pasaje de Ter 17 ■ MAP D2 ■ 928 62 23 23 ■ Closed Sun D, Mon, Tue ■ €€

Barbecued meats in a cosy rustic setting. Leave space for dessert – the rice pudding (arroz con leche) and crêpes are divine (see p62).

3 Locanda El Roque, El Roque

MAP D1 ■ El Roque 58 ■ 928 61 00 14 ■ €

Eat Italian cuisine on the end of a rock overlooking the sea. It is a culinary experience you will not easily forget.

Interior of El Belingo

4 El Belingo, Arucas

MAP D2 ■ C/Leon y Castillo 3 ■ 828 12 69 27 ■ €

El Belingo serves generous portions of classic Canarian dishes, presented with a bit more flair than the average traditional restaurant. Occasional live music is a bonus.

5 Restaurante Dedo de Dios, Puerto de las Nieves

MAP B2 ■ Ctra General Muelle Viejo ■ 928 89 80 00 ■ Closed Tue ■ €

This huge seafood restaurant is packed with lunching families at weekends. The fish soup is highly recommended.

6 Las Brasas, Firgas

MAP D2 ■ Avda de la Cruz 36 ■ 928 62 52 50 ■ €

The barbecued meats and roast chicken attract diners to this no-frills joint, where you can fill up on home cooking at low prices.

7 Las Nasas, Puerto de las Nieves

MAP B2 ■ C/de Nuestra Senora de Las Nieves 7 ■ 928 55 40 01 ■ €

Inside is cool, with marine-inspired decor, but the terrace overlooking the harbour is the best place to enjoy a leisurely lunch of prawns in garlic, or octopus and sardines.

8 Cafeteria Huerto de Las Flores, Agaete

MAP C2 ■ C/Huerta ■ 928 55 43 82 ■ Closed Sat & Sun ■ €

Set amid tropical plants in a delightful botanical garden, this is an enchanting spot in which to enjoy cake and locally grown coffee.

9 El Cápita, Puerto de las Nieves

MAP B2 ■ C/Nuestra Señora de las Nieves 37 ■ 928 55 41 42 ■ Closed Mon–Thu D ■ €

Seafood restaurants abound here, but locals insist that this family-run place outclasses the competition.

10 Terrazza El Ancla, Sardina del Norte

MAP C1 ■ Avda Antonio Rosas ■ 928 55 14 95 ■ Closed Mon ■ €

The menu may be small, but the views are panoramic at this little kiosk specializing in fresh fish.

See map on pp80–81 ←

TOP 10 Central and Western Gran Canaria

For years, the rugged central region could be traversed only by a series of tough paths, known as *caminos reales.* Today, hardy hikers continue to trek these old routes, though driving has long since ousted walking as the main way of getting about. The west of the island, however, remains largely unvisited and unspoiled. The plunging hollows nature has sliced from the towering cliffs hinder any road construction, meaning that the only way to explore this breathtaking region is on foot. Just three scary stretches of road lead to La Aldea de San Nicolás, the island's remotest *pueblo.*

Tejeda, nestled in a huge caldera

1 Tejeda

The main attraction of this town is its splendid location in the centre of the immense Caldera de Tejeda. This huge depression measures 18 km (11 miles) across. It was described by Spanish poet Miguel de Unamuno as "a tremendous upset of the innards of the earth". As well as the spectacular vistas, there is a small art gallery and two farming museums *(see pp28–9).*

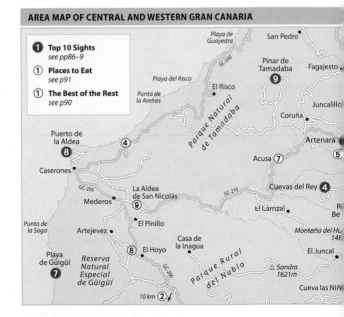

AREA MAP OF CENTRAL AND WESTERN GRAN CANARIA

Playa de Guayedra
San Pedro
Pinar de Tamadaba 9
Fagajesto
Playa del Risco
El Risco
Punta de la Arenas
Juncalillo
Coruña
Parque Natural de Tamadaba
Puerto de la Aldea 8
4
Artenara
Acusa 7
5
Caserones
GC-200
La Aldea de San Nicolás 9
GC-210
Cuevas del Rey 4
Mederos
El Carrizal
R
Be
Punta de la Soga
Artejevez
El Pinillo
Casa de la Inagua
Montaña del H 148
Playa de Güigüí 7
El Hoyo 8
Reserva Natural Especial de Güigüí
El Juncal
Parque Rural del Nublo
△ Sandra 1621 m
Cueva las Niñ
10 km 2

View over the clouds at Pico de las Nieves, Gran Canaria's highest peak

2 Pico de las Nieves

The island's highest point naturally offers impressive vistas, if you can only get there before the clouds do. After winter snowfalls, the area is swamped with islanders wanting to get a brief glimpse of the white stuff. The area is also known as Pozo de las Nieves ("Well of the Snows"): nearby, there is an abandoned well once used to collect snow, which was then taken to the capital for food preservation *(see p28)*.

3 Ermita de la Virgen de la Cuevita

MAP C3 ■ No disabled access

Artenara is one of the few places to have maintained the tradition of inhabiting caves, and tourists can stay in an adapted grotto. Although the main church is an impressive 19th-century construction, the chapel closest to the hearts of the locals is the Ermita de la Virgen de la Cuevita. Gouged out of a cliff face, the chapel has few religious images other than the statue of the Virgen de la Cuevita ("Madonna of the Little Cave"). Oddly enough, she is the patron of both cyclists and Canarian folklore groups. To reach the chapel, follow the signs from the main square for the 10-minute uphill walk *(see p47)*.

Ermita de la Virgen de la Cuevita

4 Roque Bentayga and Cuevas del Rey

Although best known as a place of worship and possibly a royal residence, this stumpy rock was also a stronghold, playing its part in delaying the Conquest *(see p28)*.

5 Cruz de Tejeda

This large, intricately carved crucifix of grey-green stone marks the notional – though not the precise geographical – centre of the island. These days, all roads meet here, but for centuries this was a junction only of the *caminos reales*, the network of "king's highways" that once crisscrossed the island. Most of the paths are still well maintained, offering dramatic mountain hikes. These include a lush downhill walk to Teror, various routes around the island's centre, and a tough trek to Puerto de las Nieves on the coast *(see p29)*.

Detail of the Cruz de Tejeda stone crucifix

6 Teror

This charming and historically important town offers the island's very best examples of traditional architecture, and is also home to the impressive Basílica de Nuestra Señora del Pino *(see pp24–7)*.

7 Playa de Güigüí
MAP A4

For those who complain that Gran Canaria's beaches are too built up and crowded, a trip to Güigüí is in order. Its fine, dark sand is flanked by looming cliffs, creating a breathtaking sight. You will have earned your day of sunbathing and relaxation by the time you arrive here. Engineers have yet to tunnel through the west coast cliffs, so the only way to get to Güigüí is on foot or by boat. Two hikes, from Puerto de la Aldea and Tasartico, reach the beach. Neither is easy, but, at two hours, the latter is considerably shorter. A hardy fisherman in Puerto de la Aldea takes groups of up to 20 people to the beach, but it's not cheap, and rough seas often prevent the trip. Be aware that if conditions worsen, he will not be able to collect you, leaving you no alternative but to hike back.

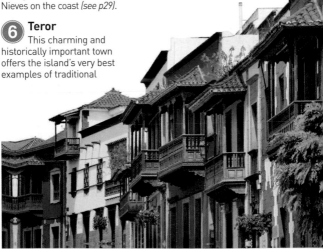

The traditional, brightly coloured architecture of historic Teror

Peaceful Puerto de la Aldea

8 Puerto de la Aldea
MAP A3

Many say that it is the travelling, not the arriving, that makes the west coast noteworthy, but Puerto de la Aldea is a lovely place to recharge your batteries before continuing along the relentlessly winding roads. For most of the year it's eerily quiet, but you might find a bit of life in the small fishing harbour or one of the excellent seafood restaurants. The small pine wood also warrants a look, as do the pre-Hispanic sites known as Los Caserones. The town becomes more animated on 11 September each year during the Fiesta del Charco, when locals go to the lagoon (charco) at the far end of the beach and try to catch fish with their bare hands (see p69).

9 Pinar de Tamadaba

The island's largest pine forest offers some welcome respite from the bustling towns and busy roads. You could stop at the picnic area for lunch, or perhaps make the 30-minute walk from the Casa Forestal to the area's highest point, at 1,440 m (4,720 ft) (see p49).

10 Roque Nublo

It's easy to see why the Guanches revered the looming form of this 80-m (260-ft) monolithic volcanic rock, especially when it's seen up close (see p28).

ABOVE THE CLOUDS IN CENTRAL AND WESTERN GRAN CANARIA

▶ MORNING

This is a full-day drive, so you will need to set out early and take some warm layers. Start off by taking in **Teror**'s important church and museum, before heading for nearby **Valleseco**. The town itself doesn't really warrant a stop, but the lush ravines certainly do (see p90). From here, follow the road to **Artenara** (see p90), stopping en route to admire the astounding **Caldera de Los Pinos de Gáldar** (see p57).

In Artenara, follow the short walk to see the **Ermita de la Virgen de la Cuevita** (see p87). Follow the road southeast to **Cruz de Tejeda**, where you can enjoy lunch at **Asador Grill de Yolanda** (see p91).

AFTERNOON

It's mountain roads all the way now, as you take the road south. If it's a clear day, stop at **Mirador Degollada de la Becerra** (see p57) to take in views of Mount Teide and Roque Bentayga before continuing to **Pico de las Nieves** (see p87), where you can park and walk to the peak. It's about a kilometre each way, so allow at least an hour and a half in total for what promises to be the high point of the day. Backtrack to the GC-600 and continue your circuit, stopping to take in views of **Roque Nublo,** if it's not hiding in its trademark cloud. Stay with the GC-60, as it snakes its way through amazing scenery, all the way to pretty **Tejeda** (see p86) to end the day with coffee and an almond cake.

See map on pp86–7 ◀

The Best of the Rest

 Mercadillo, Vega de San Mateo

MAP D3 ▪ C/Antonio Perera Rivero ▪ Open 8am–8pm Sat, 8am–3pm Sun

Of the numerous *mercadillos* (farmers' markets) held around the island, Vega de San Mateo's offers the very best selection of goods *(see p65)*.

 La Cantonera, Vega de San Mateo

MAP D3 ▪ Avda Tinamar ▪ Open 10am–4pm Mon–Sat ▪ Adm

La Cantonera is the island's largest ethnographic museum, set in a captivating 17th-century house, with over 12,000 exhibits including furniture, handicrafts and tools.

 Ayacata

MAP D3

Villages don't come any prettier than this one, especially in February, when the trees are ablaze with pale pink almond blossom. Stop for a coffee and some delicious marzipan.

 Andén Verde

MAP B3

"Green Platform" is the rather inapt name given to this bewitching stretch of stark cliffs, which tower above the ocean. Don't miss views from the Mirador del Balcón *(see p57)*.

 Valleseco

MAP D2

Offering wonderfully unspoilt natural beauty, Valleseco is known for its quality wooden handicrafts and unparalleled hiking trails.

 Fontanales

MAP D2

The first sight to greet you on arrival in this friendly *pueblo* is the church. For refreshment, drop in at Restaurante Grill Sibora, a rustic restaurant favoured by Moya locals and by city-dwellers looking for an escape.

 Acusa

MAP C3

The Acusa flatlands make a rather odd sight amid the craggy central mountains, and provide a superlative place to take a photograph of the famous Roque Nublo *(see p28)*.

8 **Cactualdea**

MAP B3 ▪ Carretera del Hoyo ▪ 928 89 12 28 ▪ Open 10am–6pm daily ▪ Adm

The arid west of the island is not known for its plant life, but the climate is ideal for growing cactuses. More than 1,200 species thrive in this lovely private garden.

9 **Old Quarter, La Aldea de San Nicolás**

MAP B3

Few travellers venture to Gran Canaria's forgotten town; fewer still find its atmospheric old quarter, east of the church *(see p40)*.

 Caldera de los Marteles

MAP D3 ▪ GC-130

It's not unusual to see livestock grazing at the bottom of this pine-fringed volcanic crater. Enjoy fine views of Valsequillo and the capital.

The beautiful landscape around Valleseco

Places to Eat

PRICE CATEGORIES

For a three-course meal for one with half a bottle of wine (or equivalent meal), taxes and extra charges.

€ under €30   €€ €30–€50   €€€ over €50

1 Asador Grill de Yolanda, Cruz de Tejeda

MAP D3 ▪ C/Cruz de Tejeda ▪ 928 66 62 76 ▪ €€

Come here for the friendliest service on the island and huge servings of meat. Try the sweet blood-sausage croquettes, a house speciality and much tastier than they perhaps sound.

2 Restaurante La Oliva, Playa de Tasarte

MAP A4 ▪ 928 89 43 58 ▪ Lunch only ▪ Closed Mon ▪ €

One of a very few restaurants on the west coast, La Oliva overlooks the sea and serves superb, fresh seafood.

3 Restaurante Arcos de La Laguna, Valleseco

MAP D2 ▪ Carretera 21 ▪ 928 61 82 79 ▪ €€

The rolling green hills of the "Dry Valley" provide an unforgettable backdrop for a meal that is big on seasonal produce. The eatery also regularly offers special menus.

4 El Encuentro, Teror

MAP D2 ▪ Plaza Del Pino ▪ 928 61 37 86 ▪ Closed Mon ▪ €€

A traditional restaurant in an elegant colonial building on a picturesque plaza opposite Teror's basilica. Prices are slightly higher than in the average Canarian restaurant, but the portions are big, and the setting is delightful.

5 Restaurante La Cilla, Artenara

MAP C3 ▪ Camino La Silla 3 ▪ 609 16 39 44

An 80-m (260-ft) tunnel entrance leads to a sun terrace with the best views of any restaurant on the island.

6 Grill El Pesebre, Teror

MAP D2 ▪ C/El Mesón 35 ▪ 928 61 37 46 ▪ Closed Mon ▪ €€

A vibrant venue for traditional dishes, including enormous platefuls of grilled pork, beef and chicken. Sit inside or on the garden terrace.

7 Restaurante Marmitia, Cruz de Tejeda

MAP D3 ▪ Cruz de Tejeda ▪ 928 01 25 00 ▪ €€€

A hotel restaurant with elegant dining and magnificent views of the pine forest. The menu features local specialities with a creative twist.

Interior of Restaurante Marmitia

8 Casa Del Caminero, Tejeda

MAP C3 ▪ Avda Los Almendros 5 ▪ 609 16 69 61 ▪ Closed Mon & Tue ▪ €€

A lovely quirky restaurant. As well as enjoying a great meal, you could leave with one of the owner's paintings.

9 Dejaté Llevar, Tejeda

MAP C3 ▪ C/Doctor Domingo Hernandez Guerra 25, Tejeda ▪ 928 66 62 81 ▪ Closed Mon & Tue ▪ €

A stylish, friendly restaurant, serving delicious international dishes, including vegetarian options.

10 El Prado, Valleseco

MAP D2 ▪ C/Alcalde Vicente Arencibia 7 ▪ 928 61 83 07 ▪ Closed Mon & Tue ▪ €

Only the freshest ingredients are used here. Try any of the Canarian stews.

See map on pp86–7

⭐10 Eastern Gran Canaria

The east of the island may appear to be something of an industrial wasteland, but away from the GC-1 motorway lie some of the island's oldest towns, harbouring delightful historical centres. But the area's history doesn't start with the Conquest. This was the most densely populated region in Guanche times, a fact made clear by the varied aboriginal settlements scattered throughout the windswept hill tops and jagged ravines.

Café sign in Aguimes' Old Quarter

AREA MAP OF EASTERN GRAN CANARIA

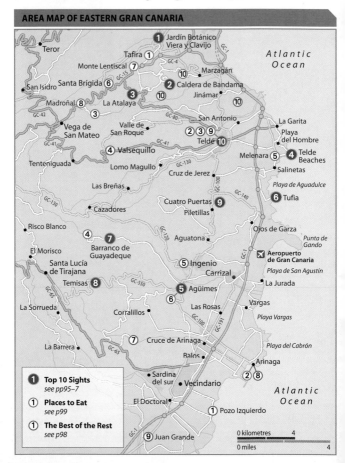

Teror

Tafira ①

① Jardín Botánico Viera y Clavijo

Atlantic Ocean

Monte Lentiscal ⑦

Marzagán

San Isidro

Santa Brígida ⑥

② Caldera de Bandama

Madroñal ⑧

La Atalaya ③

Jinámar

③

San Antonio

La Garita

Vega de San Mateo

Valle de San Roque

②③⑨

Playa del Hombre

Telde ⑩

④ Telde Beaches

Tenteniguada

④ Valsequillo

Melenara ⑤

Lomo Magullo

Cruz de Jerez

Salinetas

Las Breñas

Playa de Aguadulce

Risco Blanco

Cazadores

Cuatro Puertas ⑨

Piletillas

⑥ Tufia

④

⑦

Barranco de Guayadeque

Aguatona

Ojos de Garza

El Morisco

Punta de Gando

Santa Lucía de Tirajana

⑤ Ingenio

✈ Aeropuerto de Gran Canaria

Temisas ⑧

Carrizal

Playa de San Agustín

La Sorrueda

⑤ Agüimes

La Jurada

⑥

Corralillos

Las Rosas

Vargas

Playa Vargas

La Barrera

⑦ Cruce de Arinaga

Playa del Cabrón

Balos

Arinaga

Sardina del sur

②⑧

Vecindario

Atlantic Ocean

El Doctoral

① Pozo Izquierdo

① **Top 10 Sights** *see pp95–7*

① **Places to Eat** *see p99*

① **The Best of the Rest** *see p98*

⑨ Juan Grande

0 kilometres   4

0 miles   4

Previous pages Painted houses in Las Palmas

1 Jardín Botánico Viera y Clavijo

Gloriously fresh air and, apart from the sound of birdsong, almost total silence provide the perfect escape from the buzz of the city or the tiring mountain roads (see pp18–19).

Greenery in the Caldera de Bandama

2 Caldera de Bandama
MAP E3

The Guanche considered this crater an extinct volcano a fine place to live. Today, the striking crater offers a fine day trip for hikers, nature lovers and wine enthusiasts – the volcanic soil is perfect for growing vines, and bodegas line the approach road to the crater.

3 La Atalaya
MAP E3

The best way to see one of the island's oldest troglodyte settlements is simply to get lost in its narrow, winding streets. It is difficult to spot the cave homes nowadays, as their owners have usually added rather unsightly extensions. However, if you peek through an open door, you'll see the village's cave origins. Don't miss a visit to Ecomuseo Casa-Alfar Panchito, the cave home and workshop of La Atalaya's most famous potter (see p45). Next door is a workshop where local craftsmen produce traditional ceramics, which make excellent souvenirs.

4 Telde Beaches
MAP F3

Telde's town hall has maximized the appeal of the east-coast beaches by building a 4-km (2-mile) promenade, a lovely coastal walk. Starting in Las Salinetas, you progress to Playa de Melenara. There are some excellent fish restaurants here. Next you pass some low, pretty houses and the harbour at Taliarte; Cofradía de Pescadores is the place to go for cheap and tasty fish. Past the lighthouse, the walk briefly leaves the coast to skirt an ugly government building. There then follows a stretch with natural rock pools and rough seas. Playa del Hombre's waters are favoured by daring surfers, while beginners prefer Playa del Hoya del Pozo. Playa La Garita is a pleasant strip of black sand lapped by calm seas. The fried octopus served at Casa Santiago is divine. Just behind the beach is a taxi rank, so you need not retrace your steps.

Beachgoers on Playa del Hombre

Whitewashed houses line the cliff face at Tufia

5 Old Quarter, Agüimes
MAP E4

Agüimes was founded in 1487. Already densely populated before the Europeans arrived, it was one of the first post-Conquest settlements. These days, it's hardly a hectic town, as the tourism boom has tempted many inhabitants to the coast; but the lack of traffic and modern build-ings is precisely what gives Agüimes its charm. A mishmash of traditional and Neo-Classical architecture lines the quiet paved streets, with the crowning glory being the Parroquia de San Sebastián. As well as a top-notch restaurant (see p99), there is a delightful museum of local history (see p44).

A street in Agüimes' Old Quarter

6 Tufia
MAP F3 ■ Exit 13 from GC-1 ■ Guanche sites: entry by appointment only; call 928 21 94 21 ext 4441 (Cabildo); no disabled access

Intriguingly, no one knows exactly when the Guanche sites in this hilltop settlement were constructed. One thing that can be said of Tufia is that it seems to belong to two different epochs. A group of natural caves just above sea level served as home to primitive dwellers, but the low stone houses crowning the cliff were perhaps the work of a more developed society. Ideally located for spotting unwanted visitors, the village is surrounded by what appears to be a protective wall, suggesting that its people had some knowledge of defensive strategies (see also pp42–3).

7 Barranco de Guayadeque
Step back in time in the island's deepest ravine, once heavily populated by Guanches but now home to just a handful of cave dwellers (see pp32–3).

8 Temisas
MAP E4 ■ GC-550

A visit to this hamlet is a must for its gorgeous location and buildings. This is the best place to admire traditional rural architecture. The nearby olive grove brings income to the village; it is the island's only producer of olive oil, though it's surprisingly difficult to find anywhere to buy it here.

ALTERNATIVE ENERGY

Ask anyone here what is the worst thing about living on the east of the island and they are likely to come up with the same response: the wind. Even if you don't venture out of your car, you'll notice it. The palm trees here all lean eastward, and women avoid wearing skirts. Windsurfers, of course, are happy with the bracing conditions, along with a group of scientists. Elegant wind turbines are a familiar sight on the eastern landscape, and the Canarian Institute of Technology continues to investigate further applications of wind power.

The atmospheric Cuatro Puertas

⑨ Cuatro Puertas
MAP F3 ■ Access from the GC-100 between Telde and Ingenio ■ No disabled access

The main cave takes its name from its four entrances. Without doubt the most impressive man-made caves on the island, the dwellings are connected by short tunnels, so it is fun to explore. There is also a rare example of an *almogarén*, a series of small channels probably used for making offerings to the gods.

⑩ San Francisco, Telde
MAP F3

If you follow a narrow street opposite the museum, you will find a real jewel, Telde's historical quarter. Some of the island's oldest buildings line the tranquil plazas, hidden away in the labyrinth of cobbled alleys. Make sure you look in on the simple Iglesia Conventual de San Francisco, which houses a splendid Baroque stone altarpiece.

A DAY IN THE EAST

▶ MORNING

Once you've had a chance to stock up on **Santa Brígida**'s wines *(see p98)*, head to **La Atalaya** *(see p95)* to buy some traditional ceramics. Then make the round trip to the awesome **Caldera de Bandama** *(see p95)*, allowing at least an hour if you intend to explore on foot. Take the GC-80 to **Telde** *(see p95)*, and wander around the old town. You can delve into the region's history at **Cuatro Puertas** on the GC-100. Carry on to **Ingenio** *(see p98)*, stopping at the Museo de Piedras to buy local crafts. The town centre here is worth a look, but a better option for lunch is the **Barranco de Guayadeque** *(see pp32–3)*, with its cave restaurants and scenic picnic sites. Allow an hour to drive along the ravine.

AFTERNOON

The next stop is **Agüimes**, with its cathedral-like church and interesting history museum. From here, it is a winding drive to pretty **Temisas**, overlooking the Barranco del Polvo. After soaking up the atmosphere of one of the island's last traditional hamlets, you can either backtrack past Agüimes and onto the GC-1, or continue past **La Sorrueda**, taking the GC-65 to meet the main motorway. Whizz north to **Playa de Salinetas**, leave your car, and enjoy an easy walk along the coast. The beachside bars at **Playa de Melenara** are good for a drink before you continue your stroll to **Playa de la Garita**.

See map on p94 ←

The Best of the Rest

Windsurfer at Pozo Izquierdo

1 Pozo Izquierdo
MAP E5

A great spot for windsurfers – experts from across the globe congregate here in summer for the championships.

2 Basílica de San Juan Bautista, Telde
MAP F3 ■ Plaza de San Juan ■ 928 69 02 85 ■ Open 9am–12:30pm, 5–8pm daily

Begun in 1519, this is one of the island's oldest churches. It has continuously evolved since then; the Neo-Gothic towers were added early last century (see p46).

3 Casa-Museo León y Castillo, Telde
MAP F3 ■ C/León y Castillo 43–5 ■ 928 69 13 77 ■ Open 9am–8pm Mon–Fri, 10am–8pm Sat, 10am–1pm Sun ■ www.fernandoleonycastillo.com

Politician Fernando de León y Castillo and his engineer brother Juan grew up in this lovely house, which is also of interest as a perfect example of *mudéjar* architecture.

4 Valsequillo Villages
MAP E3

The villages surrounding Valsequillo ooze character, and if you drive northeast from the village towards Cuevas Blancas, you'll see wild olive trees and the pretty San Roque palm grove of Canary Island Date Palms.

5 Old Quarter, Ingenio
MAP E4

Penetrate Ingenio's ugly urban sprawl and you will find its peaceful historic centre. The town is particularly well known for its crafts.

6 Wine Tasting in Santa Brígida
MAP E3

Santa Brígida is the island's wine district. Most *bodegas* don't hold official tasting sessions, but they will let you try before you buy.

7 Letreros de Balos
MAP E4 ■ Dirt track off GC-104 between Cruce de Arinaga and Corralillos ■ 928 21 94 21 ext 4441 ■ Visits by appointment only

The cave drawings in the Balos ravine are considered the most important in the islands.

8 Arinaga
MAP F5

Although skirted by an unsightly industrial estate, this small fishing village has plenty of charm.

9 Juan Grande
MAP E5

Fans of historic buildings will enjoy a visit to Juan Grande, home to a rather ramshackle mansion and church.

10 Golf
Real Club de Golf de Las Palmas: MAP F3; Ctra de Bandama s/n, Sta Brígida; 928 684 890; www.realclub degolfdelaspalmas.com ■ El Cortijo Golf Center: MAP E3; Autovía del Sur, km 6.4, Telde; 928 35 01 04

Spain's first golf club was originally located in Las Palmas, but moved to a new site at the more prestigious Bandama. Nearby is another fine course, El Cortijo. Both are open to non-members on weekday mornings.

Places to Eat

PRICE CATEGORIES

For a three-course meal for one with half a bottle of wine (or equivalent meal), taxes and extra charges.

€ under €30   €€ €30–€50   €€€ over €50

1 El Lentiscal, Tafira
MAP E2 ■ Carretera a Tafira Alta 81 ■ 928 07 97 23 ■ Closed Mon–Wed, Sun D ■ €€

Traditional Gran Canaria specialities are beautifully prepared and creatively presented in this lovely old building, with its romantic corners. Tricky to find, but worth it.

2 Nelson, Arinaga
MAP F5 ■ Avda Polizón 47, Playa de Arinaga ■ 928 18 08 60 ■ Closed Mon ■ €€€

The area's most noted seafood restaurant is equally well known for its extensive wine list. Select the catch of the day and enjoy magnificent ocean views from the terrace.

Interior of Bernadino, Santa Brigida

3 Bernadino, Santa Brigida
MAP E3 ■ Cruz del Gamonal 150 ■ 928 64 13 15 ■ Closed Mon–Wed ■ €

A Canarian restaurant with lovely views over the countryside. Hearty dishes include local specialities such as *carajacas* (fried liver).

4 Restaurante Vega, Barranco de Guayadeque
MAP E4 ■ Montaña de las Tierras ■ 928 17 20 65 ■ Closed Mon ■ €

Dine out with a difference: the restaurant is inside a cave in the Barranco de Guayadeque.

One of the most popular dishes on the menu is whole piglet cooked on a bed of salt.

5 Casa Perico, Melenara
MAP F3 ■ C/Luis Morote 9, Playa de Melenara ■ 928 13 30 13 ■ Closed Wed ■ €

This restaurant is an institution when it comes to fresh fish and seafood and it is the place to try Canarian speciality *gofio* (see p63).

6 Señorío de Agüimes, Agüimes
MAP E4 ■ C/Juan Ramón Jiménez ■ 686 73 41 38 ■ Closed Sun D ■ €

Excellent Canarian cuisine served in an enchanting early-1900s building.

7 Satautey, Monte Lentiscal
MAP E2 ■ C/Real de Coello 2 ■ 828 01 04 21 ■ €€

Appetizers and desserts stand out at the Hotel Escuela's smart dining room. The combination starter is a great way to try a mouthful of many of the island's traditional dishes.

8 Casa Martell, Madroñal
MAP E3 ■ Ctra del Centro Madroñal 55 ■ 928 64 12 83 ■ €€

Set in one of the oldest houses in Madroñal, Casa Martell has been plying the locals with good food and fine wine for three generations.

9 La Tunera, Telde
MAP F3 ■ C/Betancor Fabelo 17, San Gregorio ■ 928 69 13 63 ■ Closed Sun ■ €€

The contemporary menu is here small but perfectly formed, featuring a creative take on Canarian favourites.

10 Restaurant Bodegón, Caldera de Bandama
MAP E3 ■ Carretera de los Hoyos 226 ■ 928 35 57 58 ■ €

This hotel-restaurant is set inside a converted stone barn surrounded by vineyards and olive groves.

See map on p94 ←

TOP 10 Southern Gran Canaria

For centuries, the arid coast of the south was virtually uninhabited, until holidaymakers discovered its perfect climate and fine golden beaches and began arriving in their droves. Since the start of the 21st century the region has been shaking off its package-holiday image and has invested in more chic and upmarket developments, but it's still the place for fun, sun and nightlife.

The church of San José in the historic village of Fataga

1 Fataga
MAP F4

Fataga manages to retain its charm despite the ever-growing number of visitors. The cluster of restaurants on the main road still offers good Canarian cuisine, and there is a bodega, which sells the only wine produced in the south. After visiting the small church, San José, wander around the labyrinth of cobbled passageways and look out over the ravine that shares the village's name.

AREA MAP OF SOUTHERN GRAN CANARIA

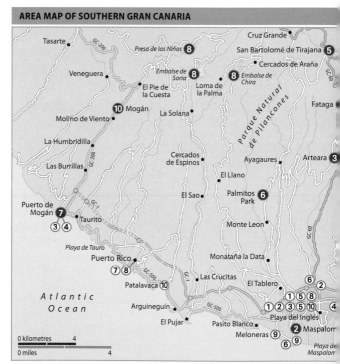

The incredible sand dunes of Maspalomas stretching towards the ocean

2 Maspalomas

The extensive sand dunes and palm-fringed lagoon set this tourist resort apart *(see pp20–21)*.

3 Arteara

MAP D5 ■ Information centre: 928 77 15 50 (book for guided tour) ■ Open 10am–4pm Mon–Fri

Although the graves have long since been looted, this Guanche cemetery – the largest in Gran Canaria, located next to the tiny hamlet of Arteara – remains an important stop on a tour of the island's sites of archeological interest. Information panels explain the burial mounds, and there's also an information centre on the life and death of Gran Canaria's earliest inhabitants. The site was once encircled by a low stone wall, remnants of which can still be seen dotted about today *(see p43)*.

4 Sioux City Park

MAP D5 ■ Barranco del Aguilar, San Agustín ■ 928 76 25 73 ■ Adm ■ www.siouxcitypark.es

There is plenty of interactive family fun and lots of yee-haws at this Wild West set, complete with cowboy action on horseback, a saloon, line dancing and even a staged bank robbery. Shows are held regularly throughout the day. In addition, you can hire horses, and there's also a small zoo, where you can get up close to some of the animals. Free buses run from the main southern resorts (see the website for details).

Map:
Guayadeque
Ingenio
na
Santa Lucía de Tirajana
GC-550
Agüimes
Corralillos
Embalse de La Sorrueda
Cruce de Arinaga
GC-65
Barrera
Sardina del Sur
Vecindario
Aldea Blanca
GC-1
El Guincho
El Doctoral
Juan Grande
Sioux City Park
GC-1
GC-500
Castillo del Romeral
Bahía Feliz
stín

Wild West theme park, Sioux City

5 San Bartolomé de Tirajana

MAP D4

Suffering from something of an identity crisis, San Bartolomé de Tirajana is more popularly known as Tunte. Perched on the side of the Tirajana ravine, it's a dramatic setting for this very traditional town, which is the capital of the island's biggest borough and includes Maspalomas and Playa del Inglés. Casa los Yanes' small museum is worth a look in, and there's a Sunday morning market in the pretty plaza.

6 Palmitos Park

MAP C5 ■ Access via the GC-503 ■ 928 79 70 70 ■ Open 10am–6pm daily ■ Adm ■ www.palmitospark.es

Save money on a visit here by buying a combined ticket, which includes entry to nearby Aqualand. Originally a tropical-bird sanctuary, the park has widened its remit to include primates and reptiles, as well as mammals. The lush location heightens the impression of a tropical paradise. If flora appeals more than fauna, you will enjoy the botanical gardens, featuring both endemic and exotic plants and lauded by naturalists (see p60).

View across Puerto de Mogán

7 Puerto de Mogán

Although on the endangered list, pretty Puerto de Mogán has so far managed to avoid the building frenzy that plagues other areas of the south coast. The authorities here have opted to lodge tourists in a low-rise complex that houses fewer visitors, which is certainly easier on the eye than the towering 1960s hotels favoured elsewhere. The quiet harbour is a fabulous place to eat seafood and while away an afternoon on a boat trip. Try to arrive early, before the tourist buses break the silence and the small beach fills up (see pp30–31).

La Sorrueda, one of the island's *presas*

8 Las Presas

Soria, Chira & Presa de las Niñas: MAP C4 ■ **La Sorrueda: MAP D4**

With limited rainfall and highly porous soil on the island, water conservation is a crucial factor in Canarian life. It's little surprise, then, that the southern *presas* (reservoirs) are important meeting-places for the islanders. The *presas* attract hikers, picnickers, fishermen and even swimmers, though bathing is not strictly allowed. The south's biggest *presa* is Soria, while the most remote is Chira, and the title of most beautiful is a toss-up between the pine-flanked Presa

---

QUALITY VERSUS QUANTITY

More and more tourists visit the island each year, but the amount of money going to local entrepreneurs is slight, thanks to the rise of the all-inclusive holiday. The *cabildo* (council) is now promoting quality tourism. Upmarket resorts such as Maspalomas, Meloneras and Puerto de Mogán are slowly changing the island's image, while rural tourism is also taking off.

de las Niñas *(see p49)* and the palm-lined oasis at La Sorrueda.

9 **Santa Lucía de Tirajana**
MAP D4 ■ La Fortaleza Museum: GC651, La Sorrueda-Hoya del Rábano ■ 928 79 85 80 ■ Open 10am–5pm Tue–Sun ■ www.lafortaleza.es

The setting-off point for the walk to La Fortaleza de Ansite *(see p43)*, one of the island's most notable Guanche sites, the sleepy village of Santa Lucía de Tirajana is characterized by whitewashed houses, red-tiled roofs and steep cobbled streets. While here, visit the shops to stock up on their specialities of olives, and a concoction of rum and herbs, known as Mejunje de Ventura, which is to be sipped rather than guzzled. Make sure you visit the excellent **Centro de Interpretación de La Fortaleza Museum**, with its re-creation of an aboriginal dwelling, and the cave.

A windmill in Mogán

10 **Villages in Mogán**
MAP B4

The rural lifestyle found in other parts of the island is hard to spot in the south, where the farmers have long since moved to the coast, but it's still possible to sample traditional life near Mogán. Rustic architecture prevails here, particularly in the Moorish village of Veneguera and in the many hamlets south of Mogán itself. In Molino de Viento, retired farmers congregate under the restored windmill to reminisce.

A TOUR OF THE SOUTH

MORNING

Leave your car, if you have one, in Arguineguín, and catch the bus to **Puerto de Mogán**. Arrive early, and enjoy the peace and quiet of the island's most charming resort, before jumping on a boat back to **Arguineguín** *(see p64)*, a two-hour trip. On the way out you will pass steep cliffs and secluded beaches before reaching the rather over-built resort of **Puerto Rico**, where you have to change boats. Arguineguín is a lovely fishing town, so far immune to the mass tourism closing in on all sides. The ultra-calm waters are ideal for children, and plenty of restaurants offer kids' menus. Try Los Pescaitos, at the western end of the promenade – best for kids – or Apolo XI, on the main road, which has more local character.

AFTERNOON

After lunch, whizz along the motorway to **Maspalomas** *(see pp20–21)*. Not far from the lighthouse, there is a "camel station"; a short ride on a dromedary is the perfect way to enjoy the dunes. Allow some time to laze on the magnificent beach, then hit the road again, this time heading north.

Mundo Aborigen offers an insight into Canarian history – helpful before visiting **Arteara** *(see p101)*. You'll need half an hour to scramble over the rocks at this Guanche cemetery. Continue north to **Fataga**, where frazzled parents may appreciate the *bodega* hidden away among the pretty alleyways.

See map on pp100–101 ←

Nightspots

1 Yumbo Centrum, Playa del Inglés

MAP D6 ▪ Avda de Estados Unidos 54

The Yumbo Centre – by day a shopping mall, by night a heaving mass of drag queens and leather-clad party-goers – is the heart of the island's gay life. Size up the bars; some have firm dress codes or are strictly men only. There are more than 200 shops and bars.

2 Ricky's Cabaret Bar, Playa del Inglés

MAP D6 ▪ Yumbo Centrum, Avda de Estados Unidos 54

Open since 2000, Ricky's is the Grand Old Dame of the Yumbo. Nightly drag shows pack the audiences in.

3 Sparkles Show, Playa del Inglés

MAP D6 ▪ Yumbo Centrum, Avda de Estados Unidos 54

The stars here regularly poke fun at audience members, so leave your sensitivities at home when you head to this flamboyant comedy show.

4 Pacha, Playa del Inglés

MAP D6 ▪ Avda Sargentos Provisionales 10

The big boys of the club world rock the southern coastline with this huge multi-lounge disco.

5 Atelier Lounge Cocktail, Playa del Inglés

MAP D6 ▪ Avda de Estados Unidos 54

Smooth sophistication and artistic cocktails are the order of the day on

Views from Atelier Lounge Cocktail

the top floor of the Bohemia Suites & Spa Hotel, with grandstand views over the Maspalomas sand dunes.

6 19th Hole, Meloneras

MAP D6 ▪ Paseo Blvd El Faro

A sports bar by day, and a live music venue by night, featuring rock, Blues and soul performers. The drinks are not cheap but the music is first-class.

7 Piccadilly Music Club, Puerto Rico

MAP B5 ▪ CC Puerto Rico

Piccadilly's pub-style quizzes, games and music have been packing in the crowds for three decades. Cheap drinks and a fun atmosphere.

8 Hideaway Lounge, Puerto Rico

MAP B5 ▪ Europa Shopping Centre

With comfy seating and inexpensive drinks, this is a good bar for watching the football and enjoying the banter with locals and holidaymakers.

9 Aqua Ocean Club, Meloneras

MAP D6 ▪ Centro Comercial, Playa Meloneras

This large nightclub in front of the Hotel H10 Playa Meloneras Palace attracts a huge crowd.

10 Eiffel Bar, Playa del Inglés

MAP D6 ▪ Yumbo Centrum, Avda de Estados Unidos 54

A chic bar, with cocktails ranging from non-alcoholic to very strong, served with peanuts and marshmallows.

Places to Eat

① El Portalón, Playa del Inglés

MAP D6 ▪ Hotel Sol Barbacán, Avda Tirajana 27 ▪ 928 77 20 30 ▪ €€€

Dine à la carte or from the buffet at this chic hotel-restaurant offering a range of Basque country dishes.

② La Palmera Sur, Maspalomas

Hidden away, the adventurous dining at La Palmera Sur is worth seeking out. Off-the-wall dishes can include white chocolate soup and pina colada cannelloni (see p62).

③ Q Tal, Puerto de Mogán

MAP B5 ▪ Between main harbour and fishing harbour ▪ 928 56 55 34 ▪ Closed Sun ▪ € (lunch), €€€ (dinner)

A funky, chilled-out joint with just a few choices cooked to order. Book ahead if you want to sample the evening menu – a seven-course feast of creative gourmet cuisine.

④ Los Guayres, Puerto de Mogán

MAP B5 ▪ Hotel Cordial Mogán Playa, Avda de Canarias s/n ▪ 928 72 41 00 ▪ Closed Sun & Mon ▪ €€€

Canarian classics meet gourmet cuisine at this excellent restaurant. There's even a separate dessert room to satisfy your sweet tooth.

⑤ Novo, Maspalomas

MAP D6 ▪ C/Barcelona 1, Playa del Inglés ▪ 928 77 27 08 ▪ Closed Mon ▪ €€

Offering sophisticated dining, Novo has decor that is sleek and chic, with funky fusion food to match. The menu is select but it will still test your decision-making skills.

⑥ La Casa Vieja, Maspalomas

MAP D6 ▪ Ctra A Fataga 139 ▪ 928 76 90 10 ▪ €€

For a taste of true Canarian cuisine, you could do a lot worse than the rustic Casa Vieja. It's an authentic experience, with local food, local musicians and traditional decor.

Interior of Bamira, Playa del Águila

⑦ Bamira, Playa del Águila

MAP D6 ▪ C/Los Pinos 11 ▪ 928 76 76 66 ▪ Closed Wed ▪ €€€

Cutting-edge cuisine at the restaurant that introduced fusion food to the Canaries. Try the spinach-and-garlic mousse or the rather unusual beetroot sorbet.

⑧ Wapa Tapa, Maspalomas

MAP D6 ▪ Avda de España 54 ▪ 650 00 17 39 ▪ Closed Sun ▪ €€

Small and lively, Wapa Tapa is *the* place to go to share tapas dishes. Try the taster menu, which includes a selection of the chef's favourite tapas, desserts, water and wine.

⑨ Samsara, Maspalomas

For chilled-out dining, this Oriental restaurant offers lovely comfortable terrace sofas and an art gallery (see p63).

⑩ La Aquarela, Patalavaca

MAP C6 ▪ Apartamentos Aguamarina ▪ 928 73 58 91 ▪ Closed Mon ▪ €€

This elegant poolside restaurant was one of the first on the island to offer *nouvelle cuisine*. The duck and sautéed prawns are recommended.

See map on pp100–101 ←

Streetsmart

A pretty street in Puerto de Mogán

Getting To and Around Gran Canaria

Arriving by Air

Gran Canaria is served by **Gran Canaria Airport**, located 18 km (11 miles) south of the capital, Las Palmas, and 25 km (16 miles) north of the main tourist resorts of Maspalomas and Playa del Inglés. Buses run every 20 minutes (Linea 1) to Puerto de Mogán and stop at all the southern resorts. Two buses run every hour (Linea 60) to Las Palmas. Car-rental offices are located in the arrivals hall, and there is a taxi rank directly outside.

There are lots of cheap direct flights from Europe, especially during the peak winter months, operated by **easyJet**, **Norwegian Air**, **Ryanair**, **Thomas Cook Airlines**, **Thomson Airways** and **Jet2.com**, as well as regular flights by **Monarch**.

US visitors will have to pass through a European airport – usually Madrid or Barcelona. Onward flights to Gran Canaria take a little over 2 hours and are most frequently operated by Norwegian Air, **Iberia** and **Vueling**.

Flight time from London to Gran Canaria is around 4 hours. **Binter Canarias** and **Canaryfly** provide frequent daily flights between Gran Canaria and the six other Canary Islands. Flying time to Tenerife is just 30 minutes.

Arriving by Sea

Trasmediterranea and **Naviera Armas** both run ferry services between Gran Canaria and other Canary Islands, but only **Fred Olsen** connects all islands by ferry and runs a complimentary shuttle service from port to city and vice versa. The route to Tenerife operates six times daily from Agaete and takes 1 hour 20 minutes. A ferry service links Arguineguín, Puerto Rico and Puerto de Mogán (see pp30–31).

Las Palmas is an important stopover for cruise liners, welcoming over 650,000 cruise passengers annually.

Travelling by Bus

Global offers an efficient bus service, with good coverage across the island; check their website or download their Android/iPhone app for routes, fares and timetables. Known as *guaguas* (pronounced wah-wahs), **Municipal** services cover Las Palmas, while Global gives full island coverage. *Guaguas* that navigate the island reach even tiny *pueblos*, but services to remote areas may be infrequent, and you often need to return to a busy town for connections.

You can pay the driver for a ticket on entry to the bus. You'll need to have small change handy – locals often use pre-paid cards, so drivers don't tend to carry much cash. For travel within Las Palmas you can buy a yellow Bono card from San Telmo bus station for €8.50 – this gives you ten journeys within the city.

By Taxi

Taxis are usually plentiful, metered, reasonably priced and can be easily flagged down in the street. Journeys originating and/ or ending in the ports or airport carry a small supplement to the fare, as do unsociable hours. There are taxi ranks in all resorts and major towns, and even small hamlets often have a local number for their only taxi driver. **Socomtaxi** has baby seats available and also has vehicles adapted for use by wheelchair users.

By Car

Car rental is popular on Gran Canaria, with more than 20 companies operating on the island, including known brands such as **Avis** and **Hertz**. Local companies are **Cicar**, **Autos Canarias** and **Autos Moreno**. Be advised that some companies such as **Goldcar** are based outside the airport in an industrial estate and are accessed from there by a shuttle transfer; check before you book. You must be aged over 21 and need to show your driving licence, passport and a credit card. Most cars are less than two years old.

The island has just four stretches of motorway, all of which are toll-free.

The GC-1 connects the city and airport to the resorts of the south and southwest, while the GC-2 runs from Las Palmas to Agaete. Two smaller stretches, the GC-3 and GC-4, connect commuter centres around the capital.

Speed limits are 120 kph (75 mph) on motorways and 50 kph (30 mph) in built-up areas, unless otherwise signed. Parking laws are rigidly enforced, so don't flout them, even if the locals do, and be aware that the legal alcohol limit for drivers is 0.05% (the equivalent of a small beer).

By Bicycle

Many companies in the capital and the south offer bicycle rental, and cycling is becoming increasingly popular, with more and more lycra-clad groups, including BMC Racing Team members, winding their way along mountain passes and coastal roads (see p59). The **Cabildo** has waymarked cycling routes in place, and you can download route plans from their website. Alternatively, there are cycling clubs such as **Cycle Gran Canaria** and **Free Motion** on the island, who organize group tours for cyclists with different levels of experience.

On Foot

Getting around Las Palmas is best done on foot, although there's a long walk from the old centre of Vegueta to the beach and port, so you may prefer to jump on a *guagua*. Hiking on Gran Canaria has long been on the radar of the walking cognoscenti, and the island has been staging an annual **Walking Festival** since 2012. Well-marked routes crisscross the island (see pp54–5); many run along old merchant trails known as *caminos reales*. You can choose to do self-guided walks with official walking notes, for example **Rambling Roger**, or join a hiking group such as **Walk In Gran Canaria**. **Inntravel** does a one-week itinerant walking holiday that takes you from the mountains to the coast; you stay in charming rural hotels, while your luggage is transported for you.

DIRECTORY

ARRIVING BY AIR

Binter Canarias
w bintercanaries.com

Canaryfly
w canaryfly.es

easyJet
w easyjet.com

Gran Canaria Airport
w grancanaria-airport.net

Iberia
w iberia.com

Jet2.com
w jet2.com

Monarch
w monarch.co.uk

Norwegian Air
w norwegian.com

Ryanair
w ryanair.com

Thomas Cook Airlines
w flythomascook.com

Thomson Airways
w thomsonflights.co.uk

Vueling
w vueling.com

ARRIVING BY SEA

Fred Olsen
w fredolsen.es

Naviera Armas
w navieraarmas.com

Trasmediterranea
w trasmediterranea.es

BUSES

Global
w globalsu.es

Municipal (Las Palmas)
w guaguas.com

TAXIS

Socom Taxis
w socomtaxi.com

CAR RENTAL

Autos Canarias
w autoscanarias.com

Autos Moreno
w autosmoreno.es

Avis
w avis.com

Cicar
w cicar.com

Gold Car
w goldcar.es

Hertz
w hertz.com

BICYCLES

Cabildo
w cabildo.grancanaria.com

Cycle Gran Canaria
w cyclegrancanaria.com

Free Motion
w free-motion.com

HIKING

Gran Canaria Walking Festival
w grancanaria walkingfestival.com

Inntravel
w inntravel.co.uk

Rambling Roger
w ramblingroger.com

Walk In Gran Canaria
w walkingrancanaria.com

Practical Information

Passports and Visas

If you are a citizen of the EU/EEA, or of Switzerland, you will only need a valid passport or ID card to enter Spain and its territories. Visas are not required for stays of up to 90 days for nationals of Australia, Canada, Japan, New Zealand, the UAE and the US. A full list of countries whose citizens need a visa in order to enter Spanish territories can be found on the website of the **Spanish Ministry of Foreign Affairs and Cooperation**.

Customs Regulations and Immigration

Although part of Spain, the Canary Islands fall outside the EU for customs purposes. Duty-free allowances for tourists travelling back to the UK are 1 litre of spirits, 2 litres of wine, 200 cigarettes, and gifts (perfume, cameras etc) of up to the value of €460. If goods exceed that value, you'll pay duty and/or tax on their full value, so keep receipts.

Anyone wishing to work in the Canary Islands needs to apply for a NIE (*Número de Identidad de Extranjero*), or foreigner's identity number. Potential applicants can download a form from the website of the Spanish Ministry of Foreign Affairs and Cooperation, and will need to take the completed application to their local Gran Canaria police department.

Travel Safety Advice

Visitors can get up-to-date safety information from the **Foreign and Commonwealth Office** (FCO) in the UK, the **Department of State** in the US and the **Department of Foreign Affairs and Trade** in Australia.

Travel Insurance

All travellers are advised to buy insurance against theft or loss, accidents, illness and travel delays or cancellations. Spain has a reciprocal health agreement with other EU countries, and EU citizens receive emergency treatment under the public healthcare system if they have a valid European Health Insurance Card (EHIC) with them. Dental care is not covered, and prescriptions may have to be paid for upfront, so keep any receipts. Non-EU visitors should check if their country has reciprocal health arrangements with Spain.

Emergency Services

For all emergency services, dial 112 – multilingual operators will connect you to the relevant service.

Health

There are no vaccination requirements for Spain, and there are few serious health hazards aside from the sun. Always use a high-factor sunscreen and re-apply regularly, especially after swimming.

Tap water is drinkable, although most people buy bottled water or use natural springs to fill containers.

For minor ailments, any *farmacía* will give advice on treatments, as well as dispensing prescription and over-the-counter medications. The usual *farmacía* opening hours are 9am–1:30pm and 4–8pm Monday to Friday. Outside those hours, check the window to locate the nearest out-of-hours service.

In an emergency, head for the *urgencias* section of either of the large hospitals in Las Palmas: the **Hospital Universitario de Gran Canaria Doctor Negrín** and **Hospital Universitario Insular de Gran Canaria**. For non-urgent cases, there are clinics in every town. Generally, a *clínica* is private, while a *centro de salud* or *ambulatorio* is run by the state.

Personal Security

Serious crime is rare, even in Las Palmas, but you may encounter pick-pocketing and petty theft in some areas of the city and the resorts. Take the usual precautions: look after your bags and wallets in markets and on busy beaches and don't leave valuables unguarded in the car. Report any theft to the *Policia Nacional* and get a crime number for insurance purposes. Very little English is spoken by the police, so you may need someone to interpret for you.

Disabled Travellers

Accessibility for visitors with disabilities is still being developed in the Canary Islands, although all new-build hotels are required by law to give full access. In major resorts, most restaurants and shops also now have ramp access, and many resort beaches in the south have wheelchair accessibility. Most buses have wide access, low floors and extra space, and more equipped ones are being introduced. **SolMobility**, based in the south, have mobility scooters, wheelchairs and hoists for hire and operate adapted taxi services.

Currency and Banking

Spain uses the euro (€), which is divided into 100 cents. Banknotes have denominations of €500, €200, €100, €50, €20, €10 and €5. Coins are €2, €1, 50c, 20c, 10c, 5c, 2c and 1c.

You can exchange money at banks, *casas de cambio* and hotels. There are ATMs *(cajeros)* in all but the tiniest of hamlets, and they are the easiest way to get cash, although they do carry a surcharge.

Credit cards are widely accepted across the island, with the exception perhaps of small bars or restaurants; it's best to check before you order. When paying by credit card in stores you will need to provide ID.

Telephone and Internet

Many hotels in the Canary Islands still make a charge for Wi-Fi in rooms, but access is usually free in the lobby. Many bars, cafés and restaurants now offer free internet access, and there are multiple Wi-Fi zones within Las Palmas. As internet costs in Spain are high, consider arranging access through your local provider before travelling, or buy a SIM card that will also buy you telephone time. **Vodafone** offers a 4G prepaid SIM card for internet and phone.

International calls can also be made from a *locutorio*, a small shop offering special rates for overseas calls. You'll find internet cafés dotted around resorts and in hotel lobbies.

Postal Services

Main branches of the *Correos* (post office) are open 8:30am–8:30pm Monday to Friday and 9:30am–1pm on Saturday. Smaller branches close at 2:30pm Monday to Friday. You can usually buy stamps in newsagents, kiosks and souvenir shops selling postcards.

DIRECTORY

PASSPORTS AND VISAS

Spanish Ministry of Foreign Affairs and Cooperation
W exteriores.gob.es

EMBASSIES AND CONSULATES

Ireland
MAP P3 ▪ C/León y Castillo, 195, Las Palmas
(928 29 77 28

UK
MAP P2 ▪ C/Luis Morote 6, Las Palmas (928 26 25 08

USA
MAP P3 ▪ C/Los Martínez de Escobar 3, Las Palmas (928 27 12 59

TRAVEL ADVICE

Australia
Department of Foreign Affairs and Trade W dfat.gov.au/smartraveller.gov.au

UK
Foreign and Commonwealth Office W gov.uk/foreign-travel-advice

US
Department of State
W travel.state.gov

EMERGENCY SERVICES
(112

HEALTH

Hospital Universitario de Gran Canaria Doctor Negrín
MAP G4 ▪ Barranco de la Ballena s/n, Las Palmas
(928 45 00 00

Hospital Universitario Insular de Gran Canaria
MAP F2 ▪ Plaza Doctor Pasteur s/n, Las Palmas
(928 44 00 00

DISABLED TRAVELLERS

SolMobility
MAP C6 ▪ C/El Greco 56, Los Caideros
(928 73 55 31
W solmobility.com

TELEPHONE AND INTERNET

Vodafone
W vodafone.es

TV, Radio and Newspapers

Gran Canaria receives the national Spanish TV channels, as well as **TelevisiónCanaria**, and with digital TV you can change the language to hear programmes in their original language. Many hotels have satellite and British and German TV, while bars have extensive sports coverage.

There are two local Spanish-language newspapers, *Canarias 7* and *La Provincia*; both are good places to find out about concerts, festivals and other events. Foreign newspapers are widely available in the tourist resorts and in Las Palmas.

Several foreign-language radio stations are available, and you can find a full list of these on **Radio Station World**.

Opening Hours

Most shops open 9:30am–1:30pm and 4:30pm–8:30pm. Large stores and Commercial Centres generally open 9:30am/10am–8pm Monday to Saturday. Virtually every shop closes on Sundays, with the exception of a few grocery stores. Larger supermarkets open 8am–9:30/10pm. Banks close at 2:30pm/3pm, although main branches will have late openings one or more days a week. Banks, shops and offices close on public holidays, and local towns observe a holiday on their Patron Saint's day. Many museums close on Mondays; check individual websites for details.

Time Difference

The islands observe GMT and BST, so mainland Spain is always an hour ahead. When it is noon in Gran Canaria, it is 7am in New York and 4am in Los Angeles.

Electrical Appliances

The standard two-pin European plug is used. The electricity supply is 220 V, 50 Hz. Visitors from the UK will need an adaptor, and visitors from the US will need a converter, as well as an adaptor.

Weather

The Canary Islands are known for their year-round good weather with warm, sunny winters, and summer heat fanned by the Trade Winds, so there is no bad time to visit. Winter is the busiest and most expensive period with prices doubling over Christmas and Easter. Spanish mainlanders arrive during summer, and July and August are busy and can be sweltering. May, June and October are quieter, less expensive and less hot, so they represent good times to visit. The mountains of the interior are most likely to see rain and low cloud in January and February, and Las Palmas can experience a lot of cloud cover in summer.

Visitor Information

The **Gran Canaria Tourist Board** has an excellent website with handy visitor information on every aspect of the island in PDF downloads, videos, ebooks, useful apps and podcasts.

There are tourist offices in every town on the island and most have their own website, filled with useful, local information.

Las Palmas Ayuntamiento (Town Hall) has a helpful website that includes accommodation, restaurants, galleries and a calendar of events for the city. Other good websites include **Spain Gran Canaria** and **Gran Canaria Local**.

Trips and Tours

The **Guagua Turística** in Las Palmas is an open-topped, double-decker bus that operates on a hop-on, hop-off basis with audioguides in eight languages. It takes in all the city's main sights. Buses run every 30 minutes between 9:30am and 5:30pm.

Gran Canaria Tourist Board offers free podcast tours (in English) to 25 locations across the island, including three in the city of Las Palmas.

Dining

Like mainland Spain, the Canarios eat their main meal at lunchtime, when the *menu del día* is available, offering three courses plus water, beer or wine for around €10. Lunch is taken late, rarely before 2pm and often continuing to 4pm or later, particularly on Sundays. By late evening, just a small meal is required, so *tapas* or *raciones* are in order. *Raciones* are about half the size of a main portion, and three *raciones* between two is a decent amount. *Tapas* are more like taster dishes or hors d'oeuvres and are a fun way to try lots of different dishes. There's a *tapas* trail in Vegueta in Las Palmas every Thursday night, in which participating restaurants offer a *tapa* plus wine or beer for €2; this is as popular with locals as visitors.

Restaurant opening times are usually 1–4pm and 7–11pm, with many places closing on Mondays and occasionally Tuesdays, too. Diners arriving in the first hour of opening will find an empty restaurant, as locals eat much later than northern Europeans.

Dining out in Gran Canaria isn't easy for vegetarians, and even less so for vegans. Newer restaurants, however, are recognizing the move to a more meat-free diet and will usually include one or two vegetarian options. Salads appear on every menu, but they are often just onions and tomatoes, and if you opt for *ensalada mixta*, it usually includes tuna. The best options for finding a good vegetarian meal are to head to an ethnic restaurant such as Indian or Lebanese.

Where To Stay

Most people heading to Gran Canaria have pre-booked their flights and hotel as a package on a bed-and-breakfast, full-board or all-inclusive basis. Hotel standards vary hugely, but a recent government initiative to move the island's image more upmarket has seen a rise in the number of five-star hotels being built in the south. Rural hotels are frequently weaker on facilities, but stronger on personality.

Aparthotels are a cross between an apartment and a hotel. There are usually rudimentary cooking facilities in the room, but guests can choose to take meals in the on-site restaurant(s).

There is a vast choice of accommodation when it comes to self-catering, including characterful *casas rurales* (country houses); *casas emblemáticas* (traditional houses), which will find you ensconced in pretty cottages in the country; restored mansions; cave houses; city apartments or luxury villas. Good research is the key to finding what you want, and there are a huge number of websites to help you.

As much of Gran Canaria is a designated protected environmental area, camping outside of authorized areas is strictly forbidden and the law is rigidly enforced. There are a number of commercial camp sites *(see p117)* and eight **Cabildo** (local government) sites, which are free to use, but you have to have written permission in advance to camp at either site. You can apply online but you must collect your approval in person from the offices of **OIAC** (Oficina de Información y Atención al Ciudadano) in Las Palmas, which is open 8:30am–2pm Monday–Friday, 4–6pm Thursday and 9am–noon on Saturdays.

DIRECTORY

TV, RADIO AND NEWSPAPERS

Radio Station World
w tvradioworld.com

TelevisiónCanaria
w rtvc.es/television

VISITOR INFORMATION

Gran Canaria Local
w grancanarialocal.com

Gran Canaria Tourist Board
w grancanaria.com

Las Palmas Ayuntamiento
w lpavisit.com

Spain Gran Canaria
w spain-grancanaria.com

TRIPS AND TOURS

Gran Canaria Tourist Board
w grancanaria.com

Guagua Turistica
w city-sightseeing.com/tours/spain/las-palmas-de-gran-canaria.html

ACCOMMODATION

AirBnB
w airbnb.com

Booking.com
w booking.com

Camp sites and permission to camp
w cabildo.grancanaria.com (Spanish only)

OIAC
Oficina de Información y Atención al Ciudadano
MAP J5 ■ Calle Bravo Murillo 23 928 21 92 29

Owners Direct
w ownersdirect.co.uk

Rural and Emblematic Houses
w grancanaria.com

Trivago
w trivago.com

Places to Stay

PRICE CATEGORIES
For a standard double room per night (with breakfast
if included), taxes and extra charges.

€ under €100   €€ €100–200   €€€ over €200

Luxury Hotels

Suite Princess, Puerto de Mogán
MAP B5 ▪ C/Alcazaba 4
▪ 928 56 50 03
▪ www.princess-hotels.
com ▪ €€
A relaxing hotel with
great facilities, including
a large pool, gym and
spa. The breakfast and
dinner buffets here are
unrivalled, guaranteeing
that you'll gain a few
pounds during your stay.

Bohemia Suites & Spa, Playa del Inglés
MAP D6 ▪ Avda Estados
Unidos 28 ▪ 928 56 34 00
▪ www.bohemia-
grancanaria.com ▪ €€€
A funky 1960s-style
retro pleasure dome of
a hotel, with luxurious
suites, gourmet dining
and a Thai-style spa.
Expansive views over the
dunes at breakfast are a
definite bonus.

Hotel Riu Palace Meloneras, Meloneras
MAP D6 ▪ C/Mar
Mediterráneo ▪ 928 14 31
82 ▪ www.riu.com ▪ €€€
An elegant five-star
hotel set in subtropical
gardens alongside the
sunset strip of Meloneras,
affording stunning
views. It boasts a bold
contemporary design,
five swimming pools
and state-of-the-
art spa facilities.

Hotel Santa Catalina, Las Palmas
MAP J4 ▪ C/León y
Castillo 227 ▪ 928 24 30
40 ▪ www.hotelsanta
catalina.com ▪ €€€
This was the island's
first hotel, welcoming
tourists back in the
late 19th century. The
exquisite Neo-Canarian
building is surrounded
by the tranquil Parque
Doramas, so it doesn't
feel as if you're staying
in a city at all. Elegant
rooms, together with
excellent sports facilities
and a small spa, not to
mention a chic restaurant,
attract the rich and
famous to this, one of
Gran Canaria's top hotels.

Lopesan Villa del Conde Resort & Thalasso, Meloneras
MAP D6 ▪ C/ Mar
Mediterráneo 7 ▪ 928 56
32 00 ▪ www.lopesan.com
▪ €€€
You've probably never
stayed anywhere quite
like this. The reception
building is in the style of
an immense Neo-
Classical Canarian
church, based on the
Templo Parroquial in
Agüimes (see p46).
Around the huge, sand-
bordered pool are houses
inspired by varied styles
of local architecture.
There are superb dining
and sports facilities,
making this the perfect
place to first indulge, and
then work it all off.

Seaside Grand Hotel Residencia, Maspalomas
MAP D6 ▪ Avda del
Oasis 32 ▪ 928 72 31 00
▪ www.seaside-hotels.
com ▪ €€€
With its elegant rooms,
exquisite restaurant and
inviting spa, Gran Canaria's
most exclusive seaside
hotel is a real haven.

Seaside Palm Beach, Maspalomas
MAP D6 ▪ Avda del Oasis
s/n ▪ 928 72 10 32 ▪
www.hotel-palm-beach.
com ▪ €€€
Seaside Palm Beach is
renowned for its amazing
level of customer service.
It features retro styling by
Parisian designer Alberto
Pinto throughout, with
bedrooms decorated in
bold, contrasting colours
reminiscent of the 1970s.

Sheraton Salobre Golf Resort, Maspalomas
MAP C5 ▪ Urbanización
Salobre Golf ▪ 928 94 30
00 ▪ www.sheraton
grancanaria.com ▪ €€€
Expect quiet luxury and
sophistication from this
superb chain hotel, which
lies in splendid isolation
above the coast of
Arguineguín. It also
has fine food, a heated
rooftop pool and two
18-hole golf courses.

Spa Hotels

Eugenia Victoria, Playa del Inglés
MAP D6 ▪ Avda de Gran
Canaria 26 ▪ 928 76 25 00
▪ www.bullhotels.com ▪ €
The hotel may be less
exclusive than some of its

rivals, but its spa is one of the best equipped. Enjoy tennis and squash courts, mini golf and a gym.

Hotel The Puerto de Mogán, Puerto de Mogán

MAP B5 ■ 3E, Urbanización Puerto de Mogán s/n ■ 928 56 50 66 ■ www. hotelpuertodemogan. com ■ €

Perched at the end of the marina, this hotel has direct access straight into the ocean via steps leading from the pool terrace. The rooms have wonderful views, either of the harbour or out to sea. A compact spa and scuba-diving school round off the facilities.

Gloria Palace Amadores, Amadores

MAP B5 ■ C/La Palma 2 ■ 928 12 85 10 ■ www. gloriapalaceth.com ■ €€

The ocean view from the rooftop pool at this hotel is amazing. There are two beaches within walking distance, a large terrace, excellent leisure facilities and a thalassotherapy circuit. The staff provide excellent service, and there are some great activities to keep children happy, so that adults can really relax and enjoy the place.

Gloria Palace San Agustín, San Agustín

MAP D6 ■ C/Las Margaritas ■ 928 12 85 00 ■ www.gloriapalaceth. com ■ €€

The site of the island's first thalassotherapy centre and still one of the biggest – you'll need 2 hours to complete the full circuit. Quietly situated away from the hectic resort centre of San Agustín, the hotel is still really convenient for the beach, shopping and the casino.

Lopesan Costa Meloneras Resort, Spa & Casino, Meloneras

MAP D6 ■ C/Mar Mediterráneo 1 ■ 928 12 81 00 ■ www.lopesan. com ■ €€

The fabulous spa at this massive complex is perhaps the island's best. It's certainly the biggest, with a 4-hour circuit of steam rooms, saunas, massaging showers and, for the brave, an igloo. Many rooms have sea views, as does the vast swimming pool.

Meliá Tamarindos, San Agustín

MAP D6 ■ C/Retama 3 ■ 912 76 47 47 ■ www. solmelia.com ■ €€

If you don't want to have to leave your hotel, this is the ideal place. Rooms are bright and airy, the spa is excellent, and there are dozens of beauty treatments on offer. The adjoining casino has cabaret shows, and the restaurant is outstanding.

Vital Suites, Playa del Inglés

MAP D6 ■ Avda Gran Canaria 80 ■ 928 73 02 33 ■ www.vitalsuites.com ■ €€

Serenity reigns supreme at this intimate spa with views over the golf course and sand dunes. Accommodation is in large, bright suites grouped around peaceful, well-kept gardens. If you crave a bit more excitement, the busy resort centre is just a 10-minute walk away.

Hotel Cordial Mogán Playa, Puerto de Mogán

MAP B5 ■ Avda Los Marrero 2 ■ 928 72 41 00 ■ www.cordial canarias.com ■ €€€

A friendly hotel occupying a privileged position in the pretty resort of Puerto de Mogán. The hotel is set within subtropical gardens. It has a very sleek spa and an à la carte restaurant.

Hotel Reina Isabel, Las Palmas

MAP N2 ■ C/Alfredo L Jones 40 ■ 928 26 01 00 ■ www. bullhotels.com ■ €€€

Contemporary meets colonial style alongside Playa de Las Canteras. Head to the rooftop space for a swimming pool with a view and spa facilities including a Dead Sea flotation room and sauna.

Rural Hotels

Finca Las Longueras, Valle de Agaete

MAP C2 ■ Carretera del Valle ■ 928 89 81 45 ■ www.laslongueras.com ■ No air con ■ No disabled access ■ €

This splendid family-run 19th-century mansion with just 12 rooms is set in the stunning landscape of the Agaete Valley.

Hotel Rural Las Calas, San Mateo

MAP D3 ■ C/El Arenal 36, La Lechuza ■ 928 66 14 36 ■ www.hotelruralla scalas.com ■ No air con ■ €

This splendid traditional building in an out-of-the-way village has just six rooms, each individually decorated. Ideal if you want to explore the central mountains or just get away from it all.

Hotel Rural Casa de los Camellos, Agüimes

MAP E4 ▪ C/Progreso 12 ▪ 928 78 50 03 ▪ www.hecansa.com ▪ No air con ▪ No disabled access ▪ €

Though based in the quiet town centre of Agüimes, this is classed as a rural hotel because of its wonderful rustic interior. Formerly a granary and camel stables, it's been fully restored.

Hotel Rural Maipéz, La Calzada

MAP E2 ▪ Ctra La Calzada 104 ▪ 928 28 72 72 ▪ www.hotelmaipez.com ▪ No air con ▪ €

This rural hotel has great views of the lush Guiniguada ravine, yet it's just 10 minutes from Las Palmas. It has cosy, elegantly decorated rooms, pleasant gardens and a good restaurant serving traditional food.

Hotel Rural El Mondalón, Las Palmas

MAP E2 ▪ Carretera de Los Hoyas ▪ 928 35 57 58 ▪ www.hotelrural mondalon.es ▪ €€€

A gorgeous boutique country hotel set alongside Caldera de Bandama, with ten rustically chic and contemporary rooms set around a courtyard. It has a great on-site restaurant, organic home-grown vegetables and its own vineyard.

Parador de Cruz de Tejeda, Cruz de Tejeda

MAP D3 ▪ Cruz de Tejeda s/n ▪ 928 01 25 00 ▪ www.parador.es ▪ €€€

A luxury mountain lodgestands among the pines in Cruz de Tejeda with jaw-dropping views and an infinity pool jutting out over the tree tops. Good dining and sunsets over Mount Teide.

Rural Hotel Fonda de la Tea, Tejeda

MAP C3 ▪ C/De Ezequiel Sánchez 22 ▪ 928 66 64 22 ▪ www.hotelfonda delatea.com ▪ €€€

A former mountain hostel now converted into a lovely rural hotel, with 11 individually styled rooms, set in the heart of Tejeda village. Enjoy views over Roque Bentayga from the rooftop solarium and tuck into some great home-cooked breakfasts.

LGBT-Friendly Accommodation

Beach Boys Boutique Resort, Maspalomas

MAP D6 ▪ Avda Tour Operador Vingresor 6 ▪ 649 01 99 85 ▪ www.beachboysresort.com ▪ €

Individually styled and themed bungalows provide the setting for this popular, gay-men-only resort set in subtropical gardens with a clothes-optional swimming pool and hot tub. An iPod docking station and DVD player are available on request.

Vista Bonita Gay Resort, Maspalomas

MAP D6 ▪ C/Carmen Laforet 1 ▪ 647 32 18 13 ▪ www.vistabonita.es ▪ €

A stylish and friendly apartment complex set in a quiet suburb, a 5-minute taxi ride and a world away from the Yumbo Centre. There are just 20 duplex apartments set in gardens with a lovely rooftop pool and a good buffet breakfast. Massages are available.

AxelBeach Maspalomas Apartments & Lounge Club, Maspalomas

MAP D6 ▪ Avda de Tirajana 32 ▪ 928 76 78 63 ▪ www.axelhotels.com ▪ €€

Lively apartments alongside the Yumbo Centre with clean, bright living rooms and bed-rooms, a good shower and a small kitchenette. The pool area has music and a party atmosphere, so opt for street-side rooms if you prefer the quiet.

Birdcage Resort, Playa del Inglés

MAP D6 ▪ C/Egipto 10 ▪ 928 76 47 22 ▪ www.birdcage-resort.com ▪ €€

Although only a short stroll from the Yumbo Centre, the gay-men-only Birdcage manages to retain a small, quiet and private setting, where guests can simply relax around the pool and gardens. The hotel has super stylish suites and a great breakfast.

Club Torso Gay Resort, Maspalomas

MAP D6 ▪ Avda Tour Operador Kuoni 46 ▪ 928 94 85 19 ▪ www.clubtorso.com ▪ €€

Clothing is optional at this upmarket, gay-men-only resort, where 12 very contemporary, spacious bungalows are set around the pool, secluded from the outside world. There's a living room with iPhone/iPod docking and a fully equipped kitchen.

Hotel Neptuno, Playa del Inglés

MAP D6 ▪ Avda Altereces Provisionales 29 ▪ 928 77 74 92 ▪ www.murhotels.com ▪ €€

Rooms in this popular, adults-only hotel are bright, clean and modern, with plenty of floor space. The staff are friendly, and the place is in a great location right next door to the Yumbo Centre.

Playa del Sol, Maspalomas

MAP D6 ▪ Avda de Tirajana 26 ▪ 928 76 01 08 ▪ www.playadelsol-hotel.com ▪ €€

An adults-only aparthotel located across the street from the Yumbo Centre. The apartments are big and bright. There are limited cooking facilities, but meals are available in the hotel. It's worth upgrading to a premier room for the pool views.

Budget Accommodation

Camping Guantánamo, Tauro

MAP B5 ▪ Playa de Tauro ▪ 928 56 02 07 ▪ €

There are three camp sites in this group, one on the coast and two further up the ravine, all with good facilities and well located for the southern resorts. The pretty location has been slightly marred by year-round campers building makeshift houses.

Camping Villamar, Tasartico

MAP A4 ▪ Tasartico to Playa del Asno road ▪ 696 92 41 63 ▪ €

This friendly, well-run site in the remotest region of

the island has cabins and caravans as well as space to pitch tents. Facilities include a restaurant and bar. It's close to the start of the Güigüí hike (see p88) and a short walk from a quiet beach.

Dunas Mirador Maspalomas, Maspalomas

MAP D6 ▪ C/Einstein ▪ 928 14 18 02 ▪ No air con ▪ €

This good-value family hotel is close to Maspalomas (see pp20–21) and has enough facilities to keep everyone happy, including two pools and a full programme of sports and entertainment. Although it's a long way to the beach, shuttle buses provide easy access to and from the sand.

Hostal Albacar, Playa de Melenara

MAP F3 ▪ C/Padre Cueto 4 ▪ 928 13 15 20 ▪ No air con ▪ No disabled access ▪ €

The Albacar is situated close to Telde's Playa de Melenara, in an area of the island that tourists rarely visit. Rooms are simple, but all have TV and en-suite bathrooms. There are some wonderful seafood restaurants nearby, and it's a great place to mix with the locals and experience the real Gran Canaria.

Hostal Alcaravaneras, Las Palmas

MAP H3 ▪ C/Luis Antúnez 22 ▪ 636 22 55 56 ▪ No credit cards ▪ No air con ▪ No disabled access ▪ €

Immaculate and brilliantly run, this is a fine budget option within

the city, situated in an agreeable residential area close to the Alcaravaneras beach and not far from the city centre. Not all rooms have private bathroom.

Hotel RK Aloe Canteras, Las Palmas

MAP P1 ▪ C/Sagasta 98 ▪ 928 46 49 07 ▪ www.hotel aloe-canteras.com ▪ €

Located just off the promenade, this hotel lacks sea views, but you can smell the salt, and you're only seconds from the beach. It's a first-rate budget alternative, with professional staff and good facilities.

Hotel Villa de Agüimes

MAP E4 ▪ C/El Sol 3 ▪ 928 78 50 03 ▪ www.hecansa.com ▪ No air con ▪ No disabled access ▪ €

Once home to the town hall, this charming 19th-century building now harbours a quaint hotel with just six rooms. The superior room has a large balcony with wonderful views over the rootops of Agüimes.

IFA Hotel Continental, Playa del Inglés

MAP D6 ▪ Avda de Italia ▪ 928 76 00 03 ▪ www.lopesan.com ▪ €

The Continental is well positioned in the centre of the resort, just a few minutes' walk from the main beach. As well as two large swimming pools, there are four Jacuzzis and a great kids' pool with a waterslide. The hotel also offers good sports facilities and nightly entertainment.

For a key to hotel price categories see p114

General Index

Page numbers in **bold**
refer to main entries

Acknowledgments

Author
Lucy Corne has written in depth on the Canaries, and this is her second guide to the islands. She also works as a freelance writer, contributing travel articles to a variety of publications. When not writing, she makes a living teaching English.

Publishing Director Georgina Dee

Publisher Vivien Antwi

Design Director Phil Ormerod

Editorial Michelle Crane, Rebecca Flynn, Rachel Fox, Cincy Jose, Ruth Reisenberger, Sally Schafer, Sophie Wright

Design Tessa Bindloss, Richard Czapnik, Stuti Tiwari

Commissioned Photography Tony Souter

Picture Research Sumita Khatwani, Ellen Root, Rituraj Singh

Cartography Zafar-ul-Islam Khan, Suresh Kumar, Casper Morris, John Plumer

Gran Canaria map derived from Gran Canaria tourist board, www.grancanaria.com. Las Palmas base map derivred from Distrimapas, Spain

DTP Jason Little

Production Che Creasey

Factchecker Matthew Hirtes

Proofreader Clare Peel

Indexer Helen Peters

Illustrator Chapel Design & Marketing

First edition created by DP Services, a division of Duncan Petersen Publishing Ltd, 31 Ceylon Road, London, W14 0PY

Picture Credits
The publisher would like to thank the following for their kind permission to reproduce their photographs:
Key: a-above; b-below/bottom; c-centre; f-far; l-left; r-right; t-top

360 Bohemia: 62t.

4Corners: HP Huber 1; SIME/Olimpio Fantuz 102cra.

Alamy Stock Photo: A.J.D. Foto Ltd. 54cl; AJD images 80tr; Alan Dawson News 68tl; Alan Dawson Photography 11br, 17crb; Thomas Russ Arnestad 64cl; C.R.Davis 46tl; Canary Islands 19bl, 34-5, 55cla; Carlos Villoch - MagicSea.com 52bl; Andrew Compton 31tc; Criber Photo 69cr; Luis Cuevas 95b; Greg Balfour Evans 35tl, 54-5, 64b;

F1online digitale Bildagentur GmbH 58tl; Folio Images 61tr; Hemis 16br, 44bc, 84cl; Shawn Hempel 97cla; Werner Hinz 56b, 89tl; imageBROKER 4cla, 46b, 47tr; International Photobank 2tl, 8-9; Islandstock 44t, 96t; LOOK Die Bildagentur der Fotografen GmbH 34bl, 65tl, /Juergen Richter 69cl; mauritius images GmbH 55tr; Michael David Murphy 56cl, 57tr; Prisma Bildagentur AG 90b; Dirk Renckhoff 18clb; Keith J Smith 10cra; P Tomlins 33crb; Travel Pictures 25cb, 27cl, 61clb; travelpixs 4cr; Maximilian Weinzierl 87crb; Wild Places Photography/Chris Howes 3tl, 18-9, 32cl, 67tr, 70-1, 82cl, 92-3; World History Archive 39cr.

Atelier Lounge Cocktail: 104b.

AWL Images: Alan Copson 7tr, 50cl; Michele Falzone 22-3; Neil Farrin 11tr, 24-5; Sabine Lubenow 11cr, 41clb.

Bernadino: 99clb.

Casa De Colon: 10cl, 12-3, 13tl, 13crb, 38b.

Dreamstime.com: Valery Bareta 82br; Yulia Belousova 86cl; Eyewave 48cla; Fevredream 15tl; Freesurf69 7cr, 81t; Ramon Grosso 52t, 98tl; Raul Garcia Herrera 63tr, Iainhamer 48b, Karol Kozlowski 11crb, 29tl, 40b, 42br, 49tl, 74b, 88b; Tamara Kulikova 24bl, 28bl, 68b, 95cla; Mihai-bogdan Lazar 102clb; Emanuele Leoni 43tl; Lunamarina 11cla, 27br, 28-9, 51cr; Maigi 31crb; Mgkuijpers 49br; Juan Moyano 10br, 20-1, 51t, 101t; Paweł Opaska 4clb, 100cl; Piotr Pawinski 53cl; Pet548 59cl; Presse750 33tl, 35br, 94tl; Rosshelen 4crb; Sssanchez 20bl; Traisoon 79c; Typhoonski 41tr, 66cr, 75cl; Maria Unt 57cl; Woravit Vijitpanya 53tr; Oleg Znamenskiy 12bl, 43cr, 47cla, 101br, 103cl.

El Belingo: 85clb.

El Museo Canario: 10crb, 16-7, 17tl.

Getty Images: Daniel Berehulak 59tr; Denis Doyle 58b; Frank Lukasseck 30cla; Calle Montes 3tr, 42cl, 106-7; Adina Tovy 83cl.

iStockphoto.com: Bareta 30br; budzik 21crb; MichaelUtech 50br; NeonJellyfish 14-5; RolfSt 30-1, 96bl; Jürgen Sack 4t; 21tl.

Jardi ín Bota ánico Viera y Clavijo: 10clb.

La Azotea de Benito: 78t.

La Palmera Sur: 62bl.

Los Guayres: 105cr.

Mary Evans Picture Library: Pharcide 39t.

Museo Néstor Las Palmas de Gran Canaria: 4b, 45clb, 45br.

Parador de Cruz de Tejeda: 91cr.

Rex by Shutterstock: Jeff Blackler 40cla, 73cr, 76cl, 77cr; imageBROKER 26t, 63cl, / Siepmann 14bc, 25tl; Jonathan Player 14cl; WestEnd61 66bl.

Robert Harding Picture Library: Markus Lange 4cl; Sabine Lubenow 19tl.

SuperStock: 60t; age fotostock 65br, 73b, / Alan Dawson 87t; FLO/Science and Society 38cl; imageBROKER 6cla; Mauritius/ Hans-Peter Merten 88c; Photononstop 2tr, 36-7; Travel Library Limited 29bl; Travel Pictures Ltd 67cl.

Tourist Board of Gran Canaria: 32-3.

Cover

Front and spine: **4Corners:** Reinhard Schmid.
Back: **Dreamstime.com:** Charles03.

Pull Out Map Cover

4Corners: Reinhard Schmid

All other images © Dorling Kindersley
For further information see:
www.dkimages.com

Penguin
Random
House

Printed and bound in China

First published in Great Britain in 2006
by Dorling Kindersley Limited
80 Strand, London WC2R 0RL

Copyright 2006, 2017 © Dorling
Kindersley Limited

A Penguin Random House Company

17 18 19 20 10 9 8 7 6 5 4 3 2 1

Reprinted with revisions 2008, 2010, 2012, 2014, 2017

A CIP catalogue record is available
from the British Library.

ISBN 978 0 2412 7636 5

MIX
Paper from
responsible sources
FSC™ C018179
www.fsc.org

SPECIAL EDITIONS OF DK TRAVEL GUIDES

DK Travel Guides can be purchased in bulk quantities at discounted prices for use in promotions or as premiums. We are also able to offer special editions and personalized jackets, corporate imprints, and excerpts from all of our books, tailored specifically to meet your own needs.

To find out more, please contact:

in the US
specialsales@dk.com

in the UK
travelguides@uk.dk.com

in Canada
specialmarkets@dk.com

in Australia
penguincorporatesales@ penguinrandomhouse.com.au

*As a guide to abbreviations in visitor information blocks: **Adm** = admission charge; **DA** = disabled access; **D** = dinner; **L** = lunch.*

Phrase Book

In an Emergency

Help!	¡Socorro!	soh-koh-roh
Stop!	¡Pare!	pah-reh
Call a doctor.	¡Llame a un médico!	yah-meh ah oon ah-de-koh
Call an ambulance.	¡Llame a una ambulancia!	yah-meh ah ahm-boo-lahn-see-ah
Call the police.	¡Llame a la policía!	yah-meh ah lah poh-lee-see-ah
Call the fire brigade.	¡Llame a los bomberos!	yah-meh ah lohs bohm-beh-rohs

Communication Essentials

Yes/No	Sí/No	see/noh
Please	Por favor	pohr fah-vorh
Thank you	Gracias	grah-see-ahs
Excuse me	Perdone	pehr-doh-neh
Hello	Hola	oh-lah
Goodbye	Adiós	ah-dee-ohs
Good night	Buenas noches	bweh-nahs noh-chehs
What?	¿Qué?	keh?
When?	¿Cuando?	kwan-doh?
Why?	¿Por qué?	pohr-keh?
Where?	¿Dónde?	dohn-deh?

Useful Phrases

How are you?	Cómo está usted?	koh-moh ehs-tah oos-tehd
Very well, thank you.	Muy bien, gracias.	mwee bee-ehn grah-see-ahs
Pleased to meet you.	Encantado/a de cononcerle.	ehn-kahn-tah-doh/dah deh koh-noh-sehr-leh
That's fine.	Está bien.	ehs-tah bee-ehn
Where is/ are …?	¿Dónde está/ están?	dohn-deh ehs-tah/ehs-tahn
Which way to …?	¿Por dónde se va a …?	pohr dohn-deh seh bah ah
Do you speak English?	¿Habla inglés?	ah-blah een-glehs
I don't understand.	No comprendo.	noh kom-prehn-doh
I'm sorry.	Lo siento.	loh see-ehn-toh

Shopping

How much does this cost?	¿Cuánto cuesta esto?	kwahn-toh kwehs-tah ehs-toh
I would like …	Me gustaría …	meh goos-ta-ree-ah
Do you have …?	¿Tienen …?	tee-eh-nehn
Do you take credit cards?	¿Aceptan tarjetas de crédito?	ah-sehp-tan tahr-heh-tas-deh kreh-deee-toh
What time do you open/ close?	A qué hora abren/cierran?	ah keh oh-rah ah-brehn/ see-ehr-rahn
this one/ that one	éste/ése	ehs-teh/eh-seh
expensive	caro	kahr-oh
cheap	barato	bah-rah-toh
size (clothes)	talla	tah-yah
size (shoes)	número	noo-mehr-roh
white	blanco	blahn-koh
black	negro	neh-groh
red	rojo	roh-hoh
yellow	amarillo	ah-mah-ree-yoh
green	verde	behr-deh
blue	azul	ah-zool
bakery	la panadería	lah pah-nah-deh-ree-ah
bank	el banco	ehl bahn-koh
bookshop	la librería	lah lee-breh-ree-ah
cake shop	la pastelería	lah pahs-teh-leh-ree-ah
chemist	la farmacia	lah fahr-mah-see-ah
grocer's	la tienda de de comestibles	lah tee-yehn-dah deh koh-mehs-tee-blehs
hairdresser	la peluquería	lah peh-loo-keh-ree-ah
market	el mercado	ehl mehr-kah-doh
newsagent	el kiosko de prensa	ehn kee-ohs-koh deh prehn-sah
supermarket	el super-mercado	ehl soo-pehr-mehr-kah-doh
travel agency	la agencia de viaje	lah ah-hehn-see-ah deh bee-ah-heh

Sightseeing

art gallery	la galería de arte	lah gah-leh-ree-ah duh ah-teh
bus station	la estación de guaguas	lah ehs-tah-see-on deh wah-wah
cathedral	la catedral	lah kah-teh-drahl
church	la iglesia/ la basílica	lah ee-gleh-see-ah/lah bah-seel-i-kah
closed for holidays	cerrado por vacaciones	sehr-rah-doh porhr bah-kah-see-oh-nehs
garden	el jardín	ehl hahr-deen
museum	el museo	ehl moo-seh-oh
tourist information	la oficina de turismo	lah oh-fee-see-nah deh too-rees-moh

Eating Out

Have you got a table for …?	¿Tienen una mesa para … ?	Tee-eh-nehn oo-nah meh-sah pah-rah
I'd like to reserve a table.	Quiero reservar una mesa.	kee-eh-roh reh-sehr-bahr oo-nah meh-sah
breakfast	el desayuno	ehl deh-sah-yoo-noh
lunch	la comida/ el almuerzo	lah koh-mee-dah/ehl ahl-mwehr-soh
dinner	la cena	lah seh-nah
The bill, please.	La cuenta, por favor.	lah kwehn-tah pohr fah-vohr
waiter/waitress	camarero/ camerera	kah-mah-reh-roh/ kah-mah-reh-rah
fixed-price menu	menú del día	meh-noo dehl dee-ah
dish of the day	el plato del día	ehl plah-toh dehl dee-ah
starters	los entremeses	lohs ehn-treh-meh-sehs
main course	el primer plato	ehl pree-mehr plah-toh
glass	un vaso	oon bah-soh
bottle	una botella	oon-nah boh-teh-yah
wine list	la carta de vinos	lah kahr-tah deh bee-nohs

knife	un cuchillo	oon koo-chee-yoh
fork	un tenedor	oon te-neh-dohr
spoon	una cuchara	oon-ah koo-chah-rah
coffee	el café	ehl kah-feh
rare	poco hecho	poh-koh eh-choh
medium	medio hecho	meh-dee-oh eh-choh
well done	muy hecho	mwee eh-choh

Staying in a Hotel

Do you have any vacant rooms?	¿Tienen una habitación libre?	tee-eh-nehn oo-nah ah-bee-tah-see-ohn lee-breh
double room	Habitación doble	ah-bee-tah-see-ohn dob-bleh
with double bed	con cama de matrimonio	kohn kah-mah deh mah-tree-moh-nee-oh
twin room	Habitación con dos camas	ah-bee-tah-see-ohn kohn dohs kah-mahs
single room	Habitación individual	ah-bee-tah-see-ohn een-dee-vee-doo-ahl
room with a bath/shower	Habitación con baño/ducha	ah-bee-tah-see-ohn kohn bah-nyoh/doo-chah
I have a reservation.	Tengo una habitación reservada.	tehn-goh oo-na ah-bee-tah-see-ohn reh-sehr-bah-dah

Menu Decoder

el aceite	ah-see-eh-teh	oil
aceitunas	ah-seh-toon-ahs	olives
el agua mineral	ah-gwal mee-neh-rah	mineral water
sin gas/con gas	seen gas/kohn gas	still/sparkling
el ajo	ah-hoh	garlic
el arroz	ahr-rohs	rice
asado	ah-sah-do	roast
el azúcar	ah-soo-kahr	sugar
la carne	kahr-ne	meat
la cebolla	ceh-boh-yah	onion
el cerdo	sehr-doh	pork
la cerveza	sehr-beh-sah	beer
el chocolate	choh-koh-luh-te	chocolate
el chorizo	choh-ree-soh	red sausage
el cordero	kohr-deh-roh	lamb
el fiambre	fee-ahm-breh	cold meat
frito	free-toh	fried
la fruta	froo-tah	fruit
los frutos secos	frooh-tohs seh-kohs	nuts
las gambas	gahm-bas	prawns
el helado	eh-lah-doh	ice-cream
al horno	ahl ohr-noh	baked
el huevo	oo-eh-voh	egg
el jamón serrano	hah-mohn sehr-rah-noh	cured ham
el jerez	heh-rehz	sherry
la langosta	lahn-gohs-tah	lobster
la leche	leh-cheh	milk
el limón	lee-mohn	lemon
la limonada	lee-moh-nah-dah	lemonade

la mantequilla	mahn-teh-kee-yah	butter
la manzana	mahn-tsah-nah	apple
los mariscos	mah-rees-kohs	shellfish
la menestra	meh-nehs-trah	vegetable stew
la naranja	nah-rahn-hah	orange
el pan	pahn	bread
el pastel	pahs-tehl	cake
las patatas	pah-tah-tas	potatoes
el pescado	pehs-kah-doh	fish
la pimienta	pee-mee-yehn-tah	pepper
el plátano	plah-tah-noh	banana
el pollo	poh-yoh	chicken
el postre	pohs-treh	dessert
el queso	keh-soh	cheese
la sal	sahl	salt
las salchichas	sahl-chee-chahs	sausages
la salsa	sahl-sa	sauce
seco	seh-koh	dry
el solomillo	soh-loh-mee-yoh	sirloin
la sopa	soh-pah	soup
la tarta	tahr-ta	tart
el té	teh	tea
la ternera	tehr-neh-rah	beef
las tostadas	tohs-tah-dahs	toast
el vinagre	bee-nah-gre	vinegar
el vino blanco	bee-noh blahn-koh	white wine
el vino rosado	bee-noh roh-sah-doh	rosé wine
el vino tinto	bee-noh teen-toh	red wine

Numbers

0	cero	seh-roh
1	un	oon-noh
2	dos	dohs
3	tres	trehs
4	cuatro	kwa-troh
5	cinco	seen-koh
6	seis	says
7	siete	see-eh-teh
8	ocho	oh-choh
9	nueve	nweh-beh
10	diez	dee-ehs
11	once	ohn-seh
12	doce	doh-seh
13	trece	treh-seh
14	catorce	kah-tohr-seh
15	quince	keen-seh
16	dieciseis	dee-eh-see-seh-ess
17	diecisiete	dee-eh-see-see-eh-teh
18	dieciocho	dee-eh-see-oh-choh
19	diecinueve	dee-eh-see-newh-beh
20	veinte	beh-een-teh
30	treinta	treh-een-tah
40	cuarenta	kwah-rehn-tah
50	cincuenta	seen-kwehn-tah
60	sesenta	seh-sehn-tah
70	setenta	seh-tehn-tah
80	ochenta	oh-chehn-tah
90	noventa	noh-vehn-tah
100	cien	seh-ehn
1000	mil	meel
1001	mil uno	meel oo-noh

Gran Canaria: Selected Index of Places